BLOGS,
WIKIS,
PODCASTS,

and Other Powerful Web Tools for Classrooms

BLOGS, WIKIS, PODCASTS,

and Other Powerful Web Tools for Classrooms

Will Richardson

CORWIN PRESS
A SAGE Publications Company
Thousand Oaks, California

For information:

Corwin Press
A Sage Publications Company
2455 Teller Road
Thousand Oaks, California 91320
www.corwinpress.com

Sage Publications Ltd.
1 Oliver's Yard
55 City Road
London EC1Y 1SP
United Kingdom

Sage Publications India Pvt. Ltd.
B-42, Panchsheel Enclave
Post Box 4109
New Delhi 110 017 India

Printed in the United States of America.

Library of Congress Cataloging-in-Publication Data

Richardson, Will.
Blogs, wikis, podcasts, and other powerful web tools for classrooms /
Will Richardson.
     p. cm.
Includes bibliographical references and index.
ISBN 1-4129-2766-8 (cloth : acid-free paper) — ISBN 1-4129-2767-6
(pbk. : acid-free paper)
  1. Internet in education. 2. Educational websites. 3. Teaching—Aids and
devices. I. Title.
LB1044.87.R53 2006
371.33′44678—dc22

                                        2005033579

This book is printed on acid-free paper.

06   07   08   09   10   9   8   7   6   5   4

Acquisitions Editor:	Jean Ward
Editorial Assistant:	Jordan Barbakow
Production Editor:	Jenn Reese
Copy Editor:	Edward Meidenbauer
Typesetter:	C&M Digitals (P) Ltd.
Proofreader:	Dennis Webb
Indexer:	Nara Wood
Cover Designer:	Anthony Paular

Contents

Preface

This may look like a book about technology, but it's really a book about the connections, collaborations, and conversations that the new "cool tools" of the Web are allowing us to create. It is less about blogs and wikis and podcasts than it is about the educators behind them who are using them so creatively to motivate students to learn more deeply and contribute what they know to the amazing body of knowledge that is the World Wide Web. And the best part of it is that very few of these educators have any great technology skills. More, they have ideas and vision of what easy publication tools might do in their classrooms.

In the 4½ years that I have kept my blog at Weblogg-ed.com, I have learned more about the world, more about education, more about people, and more about myself than in my 40-odd non-blogging years, 20 of them spent as a classroom teacher. It has been a most excellent adventure that has made me understand clearly the powerful potentials of technology in schools, and why it is crucial that our teachers and students learn to use these tools and others well if we want our kids to continue to compete for the best jobs and the best lives. We are entering a new interconnected, networked world where more and more people are gaining access to the Web and its continually growing body of knowledge. And access doesn't just mean being able to read what's there; it means being able to create and contribute content as well. At first blush, that may not seem like such a big deal, but it is a shift that requires us to think seriously and expansively about the way we currently teach students and deliver our curricula.

This book has three main goals. First, I hope to give educators some context in terms of what these technologies mean for our society as well as for education. More than anything else, the fact that the new interactive Web is weaving so many drastic changes in journalism, business, and politics convinces me that its effects on education will be equally transformational. Second, this book aspires to challenge and motivate teachers to think differently about their classrooms and the potentials of the technologies discussed in terms of pedagogy and curriculum. And finally, I hope to share enough of the "how-to" needed to get teachers started using these tools right away. Luckily, the barriers to entry to publishing to the Web have come way down.

Not every educator will use every tool discussed in this book. But every educator needs to understand the potential impact of these tools, nonetheless, because our students will be using them (or newer iterations) more and more, and because the underlying concepts they are built on are tremendously important. The social connections that students are now making on the Web, the ability to share and contribute ideas and work, the new expectation of collaboration, the ability to truly extend the walls of our classrooms . . . these ideas are at the core of this new Web. As educators, it's imperative we understand the implications of these capabilities for our classrooms.

And it's also imperative that we all work to make sure that every child gets access to this new Web as well. I have been extremely fortunate to work in a district and community where the Internet is a staple. But I fully realize that few of these ideas will have any relevance to teachers and students who do not have access. Although almost 100% of schools have an Internet connection, far fewer than 100% of our kids have meaningful access. We still have a long way to go, and I would urge every educator to do whatever he or she can to insure every student gets connected to these ideas as quickly as they can.

Finally, I know that many educators have legitimate concerns about publishing student work to the Web. I've made every effort to convince you that first, sharing what students do to a wider audience is good pedagogy, and that second, we can keep our kids safe in the process. But this is not a perfect world, and certainly there will be times when our students' identities are compromised or they will act inappropriately in front of an online audience. Every teacher and every district should be prepared for that. In my years of working with these technologies, however, I can tell you from personal experience and from collecting anecdotal data from many other teachers, students don't usually abuse the tools, and that "teachable moments" rarely become something more than just that. But even if your or your school's comfort level precludes using them with your students, use them for yourself. These tools are great for professional development and collaboration with other teachers and mentors, and I urge you to embrace them for your own use even if you don't bring them to your students.

This book would not have been possible without the generous sharing of ideas of dozens of educator bloggers who have taught me more than I could ever capture in just a couple of hundred pages. And although I can't name them all, I can thank a few who have helped me in profound ways. When I first started looking for teachers using blogs, Pat Delaney was an inspiration and an early mentor. The generosity of Ken Tompkins to offer space on his server to let me experiment told me much about the goodness of bloggers. And, early on when Tim Lauer asked me up from the audience to share in his blogging presentation at a national conference, it was a moment of validation. Joe Luft, Pam Pritchard, Sebastian Fiedler, Sarah Lohnes, Terry Elliot, and Peter Ford are all early adopters whose feedback and support of my own work were and are most appreciated. Other educator bloggers like Anne Davis, Tom Hoffman, Barbara Ganley, Ken Smith, Alan Levine, Stephen Downes, George Siemens, David Warlick, and James Farmer, to name a few, are those whose work I read with anticipation each day. Finally, I want to thank Alan November, who has become a good friend and a valued mentor, and my colleague and friend Rob Mancabelli, who along with many creative and dedicated educators at my school, Hunterdon Central, have been so supportive of my efforts. All of these people and many more have inspired me and taught me about how these tools can teach and build connections and community. I'm very, very thankful to all of them and to all of the others who have contributed to this work.

The best news is that each day I find more teachers beginning to publish their thoughts, their voices, and their knowledge to this new, evolving Web. That's the power of these tools and of this new Internet that we are creating together, and it is much of the motivation for this book. My learning never stops. I sincerely wish the same for you.

Acknowledgments

Corwin Press and the author would like to thank the following individuals for their assistance:

Mike Muir
Director and Associate Professor
Maine Center for Meaningful Engage Learning
University of Maine – Farmington
Farmington, ME

Erica C. Boling, PhD
Assistant Professor of Literacy Education
Rutgers, The State University of new Jersey
New Brunswick, NJ

Karen Stearns
Assistant Professor of English
State University of New York – Cortland
Cortland, NY

Sandra K. Enger, PhD
Associate Professor of Science Education
The University of Alabama – Huntsville
Huntsville, AL

Gary M. Graves
Senior Research and Evaluation Advisor
Northwest Regional Educational Laboratory
Portland, OR

Janel D. White-Taylor, PhD
Assistant Professor
Arizona State University East Education
Mesa, AZ

About the Author

 **Will Richardson** is an internationally known "evangelist" for the use of Weblogs, RSS, and related Internet technologies in classrooms and schools. A classroom teacher for more than 20 years, he has integrated these technologies into his curricula for 4 years and over the past 3 years has spoken to thousands of educators on the merits of "The Read/ Write Web." In various Weblog projects, his students have collaborated with best-selling authors, Pulitzer Prize–winning journalists, and students in classrooms from around the world. One of the first educator bloggers, his own Weblog at www.weblogg-ed.com has been featured in the *New York Times, Washington Times, Syllabus,* and others, and it is a primary resource for the creation and implementation of Weblog technologies on the K–12 level. His articles have appeared in *Educational Leadership, English Journal,* and *Principal Leadership,* among others, and he has presented and given workshops about Weblogs and RSS and other technologies at national conventions such as the NECC, ASCD, Journalism Education Association, and many others. He is also a featured blogger at Ed Tech Insider (www.eschoolnews.com/eti) and is a regular on the biweekly "Ed Tech Coast to Coast Podcast" (www.edtechcoasttocoast.com).

Will is currently the Supervisor of Instructional Technology and Communications at Hunterdon Central Regional High School in Flemington, NJ, where he also oversees a Weblog program of more than 400 sites.

To Wendy, Tess, and Tucker.
We are family.
I love you all.

1 The Read/ Write Web

Tim Berners-Lee had a grand vision for the Internet when he began development of the World Wide Web in 1989. "The original thing I wanted to do," Berners-Lee said, "was make it a collaborative medium, a place where we [could] all meet and read and write" (Carvin, 2005). At the time, the Internet was not much more than a network of computers that researchers and government officials used to share text and data, just a small blip on the radar screens of all but the most technologically savvy. But Berners-Lee saw the potential to construct a vast "web" of linked information, built by people from around the globe, creating the ability to share not just data but personal talents and experiences in new and powerful ways.

The first part of Berners-Lee's dream came to fruition in 1993 with the development of the Mosaic Web browser. Seemingly overnight, the Internet went from a text and numbers based research tool for the few to a colorful, graphical world of information for the masses. Even though content was limited in those early days, millions of people soon started going online to read or "surf" the Web for information and entertainment. And as access spread, connections became faster, and more and more Web designers and authors set up shop, the twentieth century ended with the Internet taking its place as an essential communications and research network connecting people around the globe.

But even with that initial period of immense and rapid growth, the original vision of being able to read *and* write to the Web was slow (in Internet terms, at least) to be realized. Writing to the Web required knowledge of the HTML code that make Web pages work and of the protocols to get those pages up and running on the Internet. To be sure, there were text-based newsgroups to share ideas and some sites like Amazon.com where readers could leave reviews and opinions.

But for the most part, the ability to create content on the Web was nowhere near as easy as consuming it, and even those that could create did so with little means for easy collaboration.

A NEW WORLD WIDE WEB

Today, however, that's no longer the case.

The past few years have seen the development of a wide variety of easy Internet publishing tools that have done much to fulfill Berners-Lee's concept of a Read/Write Web. A 2003 survey by the Pew Internet & American Life Project found that more than 53 million American adults or 44% of adult Internet users had used the Internet to publish their thoughts, respond to others, post pictures, share files, and otherwise contribute to the explosion of content available online (Lenhart, Fallows, & Horrigan, 2004). At the beginning of 2006, Technorati.com, one of many blog tracking services, listed almost 25 million blogs (short for Weblogs), the first widely adopted easy publishing tool of the Read/Write Web, which people use to create personal journals of their lives, build resource sites with colleagues, or filter the news of the day for audiences large and small with no need to know how to code pages or transfer files. At this writing, the service was adding over 70,000 new blogs and a million Weblog posts *each day.* In fact, Weblogs were already so popular by the end of 2004 that the Merriam-Webster dictionary chose it as its "Word of the Year for 2004," and the bloggers were ABC News' "People of the Year." In other words, the new two-way Web has officially arrived.

And it's not just blogs: Creating content of all shapes and sizes is getting easier and easier. High-bandwidth Internet access and expanded computer memory and storage continue to grow, and developers are creating tools to publish text or photos or video or whatever else easily to the Web. We're in the midst of an explosion of technologies that will continue to remake the Web into the community space Berners-Lee originally envisioned. It's already happening in many areas of our lives, such as politics, journalism, and business. And from an educational standpoint, this new Read/Write Web promises to transform much of how we teach and learn as well.

For most, however, the significance of these changes is still just starting to be realized. We are no longer limited to being independent readers or consumers of information; as we'll see, we can be collaborators in the creation of large storehouses of information. In the process, we can learn much about ourselves and our world. In almost every area of life, the Read/Write Web is changing our relationship to technology and rewriting the age old paradigms of how things work. No doubt, these changes will take many years to process. In fact, as author Dan Gillmor writes, "the people who'll understand this best are probably just being born" (Gillmor, 2005).

EXTRAORDINARY CHANGES

The Read/Write Web holds transformational changes in store for teachers and students of all stripes. But, as is often the case, education has been slow to adapt to these new tools and potentials. In other areas of our lives, however, we can see some of these transformations happening right now, right in front of our eyes.

Take politics, for example. For Howard Dean, the 2004 Democratic presidential candidate, the Read/Write Web has already led to extraordinary changes to the face of politics. Although Dean didn't end up winning his party's nomination, his *Blog for America* (www.blogforamerica.com) altered the face of grass roots politics and campaign fund raising as we know it. With the ability to not only read about campaign events and platforms but to easily publish their own ideas and feedback as well, tens of thousands of Americans became a part of the community that discussed the major issues of the campaign through the blog. Tens of thousands more ended up donating more than $40 million dollars through the site in chunks that averaged $80. By the end of the campaign, all of the major candidates had their own Weblogs, and there is little doubt that politicians will continue to try to find ways to harness the sense of community that the Read/Write Web makes possible.

The ability to easily publish text, pictures, and video is changing the face of journalism as we know it as well. There is no better example than coverage of the heart-breaking Indian Ocean earthquake and resulting tsunami that killed upwards of 150,000 people just after Christmas in 2004 (or, for that matter, the horrible devastation caused by Hurricane Katrina in New Orleans in the summer of 2005). Within minutes of the event, links to gripping first-person accounts coupled with digital photos and video were spreading throughout the "blogosphere," providing the type of raw detail that usually wouldn't appear in the media. Wikipedia (www.wikipedia. org), a collaborative encyclopedia built on a *wiki* that anyone with an Internet connection can use to publish to and edit, became a clearinghouse of information based on the work of thousands of amateur researchers who published facts and photos and links as they found them. In recognition of these efforts, the *New York Times*, the paragon of traditional journalism, noted that bloggers "were hard to beat" when it came to early coverage of the catastrophe (Schwartz, 2004).

In reality, the Read/Write Web has created millions of amateur reporters who now have their own digital printing presses. They've also created millions of amateur editors who are, in blogging parlance, ready to "fact check your a**" whenever a major story breaks. Just ask Dan Rather, who showed what turned out to be inauthentic copies of President George W. Bush's military records during a segment on "60 Minutes" late in the 2004 campaign cycle. It didn't take long for bloggers to claim that the documents were forgeries, leading to a retraction from CBS a week later, and, some would say, Rather's retirement six months hence (Pein, 2005).

Dan Gillmor, a former reporter and blogger at the San Jose Mercury News and author of *We the Media*, puts the power of the Read/Write Web this way: "If my readers know more than I do (which I know they do,) I can include them in the process of making my journalism better" (Kosman, 2005). By including people in the process, this new Web creates all sorts of opportunities for "participatory journalism" which, of course, creates all sorts of new definitions and descriptions of just what journalism is. Two early examples are the Northwest Voice in Bakersfield, California (www.northwestvoice.com) and Greensboro [NC] 101 (www.greensboro101.com). The vast majority of articles and content featured on the Voice Website and in its print edition is contributed by residents of the community. It's "down-home news told from your perspective." In Greensboro, local Weblogs are being cobbled together to create a menu of local voices and opinions for readers to tap into. Traditional media outlets such as the *Washington Post*, the BBC, and others are scrambling to respond to this trend, creating interactive spaces for readers, buying on-the-spot news photos from people with camera phones, and running amateur video of news events. And these changes show no signs of slowing.

More recently, businesses have begun exploring the use of Weblogs and wikis for a variety purposes, from public relations to customer service to internal communications. When Microsoft began offering up Weblog space to some of its developers last year, potential customers had an opportunity to not only read about the inner workings of the company, they had a chance to respond and participate. Now, hundreds of corporations including GM, Coca-Cola, Sun Microsystems, and Apple have blogs, and many CEOs are beginning to catch on to blogging as well.

No matter how you look at it, we are creating what author Douglas Rushkoff calls a "Society of Authorship" where every teacher and every student, every person with access will have the ability to contribute ideas and experiences to the larger body of knowledge that is the Internet. And in doing so, Rushkoff says, we will be writing the human story, in real time, together, a vision that asks each of us to participate (Rushkoff, 2004) .

THE READ/WRITE WEB IN EDUCATION

For educators and students around the world, there's no doubt that the evolution of the Read/Write Web holds similarly significant changes in store. Not unsurprisingly, schools have been slower to consider the potentials of the Read/Write Web in the classroom to date. Although a considerable number of colleges and universities have begun to explore the potential, K–12 educators are just now beginning to contemplate in significant numbers the ways in which this new Internet can enhance their own practice and their students' learning. Without question, our ability to easily publish content online will force us to rethink the way we communicate with our constituents, the way we deliver our curriculum, and the expectations we have of our students. It also has the potential to radically change what we assume about teaching and learning, and it presents us with important questions to consider: What needs to change about our curriculum when our students have the ability to reach audiences far beyond our classroom walls? What changes must we make in our teaching as it becomes easier to bring primary sources to our students? How do we need to rethink our ideas of literacy when we must prepare our students to become not only readers and writers, but editors and collaborators as well? How do we best put to use the reams and reams of "digital paper" that Weblogs provide?

On first blush, the tools on this new Web may not seem well-suited to a climate of standardized test scores and government accountability. Some will see the constructionist, collaborative pedagogy of Weblogs, wikis, digital photo and video, and others as presenting a risk instead of a solution for a system whose students continue to struggle to stay apace of their international peers. In reality, however, these tools have considerable relevance to state and local core content curriculum standards, and there is much reason to believe their implementation in schools will better prepare students for a slew of new literacies and competencies in their post-education lives.

DIGITAL NATIVES

Today's schools are faced with a difficult dilemma that pits a student body that has grown up immersed in technology against a teaching faculty that is less facile with the tools of the trade. The National Technology Plan released in January 2005 went so far as to admit that "Today's students, of almost any age, are far ahead of their teachers in computer literacy. They prefer to access subject information on the Internet, where it is more abundant, more accessible and more up-to-date" (National Educational Technology Plan, 2005). Educational theorist Marc Prensky says these students are "Digital Natives" who are well versed in the uses and etiquette of computers, digital cameras, cell phones, text messaging, Weblogs, and the like. These students have been born into a world filled with gadgets and online community, and to most of them it's a way of life (Prensky, 2001a).

Take, for example, 13-year-old Matthew Bischoff, who became a "podcasting" sensation by creating "Escape from the World," a regular digital broadcast of technology-related news that he produced and posted to the Web from his bedroom (www.matthewbischoff .com/blog). Or 14-year-old Dylan Verdi, whose skill at video blogging (posting homemade videos to her Weblog) led her to be featured on the ABC World News Tonight feature on bloggers (Vargas, 2004; www.dylanverdi.blogspot.com). Or my eight-year-old daughter Tess, whose "Weather Recipes" book, which we scanned and uploaded to Flickr.com, has been viewed more than 500 times as of this writing (only 50 or so by me, I swear: www.flickr.com/photos/wrichard/ sets/96435/). All around us, kids are creating content in ways that most adults haven't yet tried.

Results of a Netday survey released in March 2005 assert that technology has become "an indispensable tool in the education of today's students." The survey showed that 81% of students in grades 7–12 have e-mail accounts, 75% have at least one Instant Messenger (IM) screen name, and that 97% believe strongly that technology use is important in education. And the fastest growing age group for using the Internet is 2- to 5-year-olds (NetDay News, 2005). According to Prensky, "this online life is a whole lot bigger than just the Internet. This online life has become an entire strategy for how to live, survive and thrive in the twenty-first century where cyberspace is a part of everyday life." And, in addition, "the possibilities for what Digital Natives can do online are growing exponentially" (Prensky, 2004b).

This immersion in technology has neurological effects as well. William D. Winn, Director of the Learning Center at the University of

Washington, believes that years of computer use creates children that "think differently from us. They develop hypertext minds. They leap around. It's as though their cognitive structures were parallel, not sequential" (Prensky, 2001a). In other words, today's students may not be well-suited to the more linear progression of learning that most educational systems employ.

Most teachers in today's schools, meanwhile, were not surrounded by technology growing up, a fact that Prensky says makes them "Digital Immigrants." And the speed with which these technologies have been developed (remember, the Web browser is only 12 years old) means there are many immigrants out there. No matter how hard they may try to adopt and adapt to these tools, Prensky says, they still carry accents: they print out their e-mail, they write checks to pay their bills, or they use phone books to look up phone numbers. Unlike their students, who seem able to tune into many different media at once, the digital immigrants don't multitask well, and the tools of the online world are rarely used personally or in the classroom.

The bad news is the Read/Write Web threatens to make these differences between teachers and learners even more acute. Whereas students are open to the ways of new technologies, schools by and large are not. Howard Rheingold, author of *Smart Mobs,* says "I make a basic distinction (one that I think is widening) between education and schooling: people, especially young people, continue to learn—and to adopt new media—but institutions, and those who run them, are much slower to change their ways" (Rheingold, 2004). All of this paints the picture of an educational system that is out of touch with the way its students learn.

The good news, however, is that the tools discussed in this book have just as much chance of closing this gap as widening it. The reason is because by their very nature, they are relatively easy for anyone, native or immigrant, to employ in the classroom. The sudden explosion in online content creation could not occur if technological barriers to entry were high, and these barriers will continue to come down as the tools themselves continue to evolve. Even more important is that most of the tools of the Read/Write Web are free and will most likely stay that way as open-source software alternatives continue to grow. That doesn't mean that it won't be work for the immigrant educators to lose those accents. But on the whole, we can be optimistic that once the potential of the Read/Write Web finds its way into schools, students and teachers will be launched on a path of discovery and learning like they have never experienced before.

THE TOOLBOX

Just what are the technologies that promise to change the way we teach and learn? It seems the number grows each day, but the teacher's toolbox that will be covered in this book is made up of a mix of those that publish, those that manage information, and those that share content in new collaborative ways. They are

1. **Weblogs**: Thousands of teachers and students have already incorporated Weblogs into their classrooms and into their practice. Blogs, as they are known, are easily created, easily updateable Websites that allow an author (or authors) to publish instantly to the Internet from any Internet connection. They can also be interactive, allowing teachers and students to begin conversations or add to the information published there. Weblogs are the most widely adopted tool of the Read/Write Web so far.

2. **Wikis**: A wiki is a collaborative Webspace where anyone can add content and anyone can edit content that has already been published. In schools, teachers and students have begun using password protected wikis to create their own textbooks and resource sites.

3. **Rich Site Summary (RSS)**: RSS is a technology that allows educators to subscribe to "feeds" of the content that is created on the Internet, whether it's written in a Weblog or in a more traditional space such as newspapers or magazines. In other words, just as in traditional models of syndication, content comes to the reader instead of the reader retrieving the content. From a research and information management standpoint, RSS may be the new "killer app" (extremely useful application) for education.

4. **Aggregators**: An aggregator collects and organizes the content generated via the RSS feed.

5. **Social Bookmarking**: Bookmarking sites allow users to not just save the Web addresses of interesting content. They allow readers to save and archive entire pages, thus producing a form of a searchable, "personal Internet." In addition, social bookmarking sites like Furl.net and del.icio.us allow teachers and students to build subject specific resource lists that they can easily share when using RSS. This in turn creates a community of information gatherers who extend the reach of any one person.

6. **Online Photo Galleries**: Publishing digital photos to the Web not only means sharing pictures with family and friends. It means becoming a part of a community of photographers sharing ideas and experiences. And, as we'll see, it means adding another dimension to what students and teacher can do with digital images in the classroom.

7. **Audio/video-casting**: New technologies make it easy to not only produce digital voice and video files, they also make it easy to publish and distribute them to wide Internet audiences. Students can now easily "write" in many different media, a fact that opens up all sorts of possibilities for the classroom.

Although this list is not exhaustive, it is a relevant sampling of the types of tools being developed and the nature of their impact.

In and of itself, the "old" read-only web was a transformative technology. It has changed the way we work, the way we learn, and the way we communicate. I would argue that historians may look back on these past 10 years the same way we look back on the early days of the printing press, the steam engine, or the automobile. The Web has changed our lives.

This "new" Read/Write Web will change it even more. As the former CEO of Hewlitt-Packard Carly Fiorina said, the past 25 years in technology have been "the warm-up act." What we're entering is the "main event, and by main event I mean an era in which technology will truly transform every aspect of business, of government, of society, of life" (Friedman, p. 216.). And, I would add, education.

This book will focus on the ways these technologies can help educators take full advantage of the potentials for personal learning with the new Web and show ways in which teachers can effectively bring these technologies to their students to enhance their learning and better prepare them for their post-education worlds. Throughout, we will discuss the pedagogies and literacies that surround successful implementation of the tools in the classroom.

KEEPING STUDENTS SAFE

Before launching headfirst into a discussion of the tools, it's important to take some time to talk about keeping our students safe on the Read/Write Web. Obviously, this is about more than not publishing children's names and pictures on the Internet or permitting students to access obscene content online, acts that federal and state laws already regulate. Safety is now about responsibility, appropriateness, and common sense as well. If we ask our students to publish, even if we know they are publishing outside of the classroom (which they are), it's our obligation to teach them what is acceptable and safe and what isn't.

Like just about everything else in life, using the Web carries with it some risks. But again, like most other things, those risks can be greatly reduced by having the appropriate information in hand and by planning. Although cases of Internet predators are usually widely reported and are heart-wrenching in nature, the actual numbers of Web-related abductions or seductions are very, very small. That should not in any way minimize, however, our efforts to provide our students with the knowledge they need to keep themselves safe.

Let's start with simply interacting with the Web. We all know that there is an overwhelming amount of inappropriate content on the Internet, be it pornography, bad language, or just bad taste.

Schools and libraries are required by the Child Internet Protection Act (CIPA) to filter content that is accessible via the Internet. In addition, CIPA requires that schools monitor the online activities of minors and to have a policy in place that addresses the "safety and security" of minors when online (CGB System Support Office, 2005). But as much as we may try to stop all forms of inappropriate content from being accessible from school, the reality is some is not filtered.

It's not hard to imagine that along with more people being able to create and publish content to the Web will come more inappropriate content. Internet filters will become increasingly hard pressed to restrict such content. For example, there are thousands of obscure Weblogs that publish questionable content that fall outside the scope of the major filtering programs. I know. I've had the misfortune of running across some of them in my travels, and my students have as well. To deal with this, schools are faced with a couple of options. First, districts can choose to block some of the large Weblog hosting sites like blogspot.com or xanga.com or myspace.com. This eliminates literally millions of sites from student access and blocks not only the questionable sites but the large majority of perfectly appropriate sites that might be relevant to learning. I know of many bloggers, for instance, who write inspiringly and educationally about their work and their areas of expertise on their blogspot.com sites, sites that some schools have chosen to block.

The other alternative, of course, is to teach students the skills they need to navigate the darker sides of the Web safely and effectively. I remember back in the days before CIPA when our classroom access to the Web was unfiltered. My students and I spent a good deal of time talking about how responsible use meant not just refraining from actively seeking out these inappropriate sites, but also reacting appropriately when they were happened upon. (We still do that today.) I'll never forget the day I was sitting in between two students as they were working on the Web when suddenly one of them let out an audible gasp. He had been researching tattoos, and when I turned to see what was on his screen, I gasped almost as loudly. (Use your imagination.) But my student reacted the way he should have; he quickly hit the back button on the browser and without making a big deal about it went about his work. Later, as a class, we talked about the incident and reinforced the proper reaction the student had. My students knew that they could not be kept totally safe from the ne'er-do-wells of the world, but they also knew they had a choice as to how they responded when faced with such a situation.

Teachers working with younger children obviously have more to be concerned about, and I would urge a great deal of planning and testing before going online. Create your own Web tours beforehand and limit the amount of freedom students have to surf. But even in the early grades, teaching appropriate use is critical. Kids are coming to the Web earlier and earlier, and it's obviously very important that we prepare them for life online.

From a content-creation and publishing standpoint, there are other issues to deal with. The first, of course, is protecting the privacy of students. Let's start with personal information. Most states now have laws that require parents to decide how much personal information about their children may be published on the school Website. Parents in my state, New Jersey, may opt to allow photos, full names, and even addresses to be published to the site. So, the first step for any teacher thinking about having students publish online is to make sure to get parental approval. The best way to do this is to send a letter home to parents clearly explaining your plans and asking permission for students to participate. That letter should include a description of the technology, how it will be used, what security measures have been put in place, and what your expectations are of your students. See the example of a letter dealing with the use of blogs at the end of this chapter. It would also be well advised to discuss your use of blogs with supervisors and administrators as well.

From a student standpoint, teachers have to be ready to discuss what should and should not be published online. Obviously, students should never reveal information about where they live, where they work, and anything else that might identify them to potential predators. This, in fact, is one of the biggest issues with the personal journal sites like Xanga and MySpace. Many adolescents who use these sites include full names, addresses, and provocative pictures of themselves, behavior that can only increase their chances of getting into trouble. In addition, students need to know that any content they create online will become a part of their Web portfolio. They need to ask themselves "What if someone finds this piece five or ten years from now?"

One of the most difficult roads to navigate in the world of the Read/Write Web is how to balance the safety of the child with the benefits that come with students taking ownership of the work they publish online. First, we need to decide who the audience is. Is it just a small peer group? The whole class? The entire Internet? As we'll see, there are ways to set the size and shape of the intended audience for what our students create. Then, we need to think about how clearly to identify who the student is. Complete anonymity is the safest route when publishing, no doubt, but it detracts from the personal achievement and ownership that a student feels in publishing her work. Using a full name can help in that regard, but it adds a layer of risk to the process. On the K–12 level at least, most teachers take the middle ground by having students use just first names when publishing. Some, however, do give the option of using a pseudonym for students who may have unique first names. Others opt for complete anonymity by assigning a number to each student to use. Either way, it's an important balance for teachers, students, and parents to negotiate.

Because most of these tools are collaborative and offer the potential to work with other students or mentors or primary sources outside of school, teachers need to think about ways to vet the people who are allowed into the process. With blogs, for instance, the ability for people to leave comments can be a very powerful and positive learning tool. If, however, there is unchecked access to commenting on a student site, it may open up the door to inappropriate or irrelevant feedback. Again, this is something my students and I would talk about. What happens if someone whom we don't know leaves a comment? What if the comment is distasteful? In my experience, the vast majority of instances in which outsiders commented on student work were positive. But teachers and districts need to find their own balance.

Today, despite the relative newness of these tools, thousands of teachers and students are using Weblogs, wikis, RSS, and the rest to enhance student learning in safe, productive, effective ways. No doubt, employing these tools is not as simple as exchanging paper in a closed classroom environment. But the learning opportunities that these tools offer makes it worth all of our whiles to create best practices in our own right.

Sample Blogging Letter from http://www.budtheteacher .com/wiki/index.php?title=Blogging_letter

Dear Families:

From now to the end of the year, Ms. Tammy's class will be taking part in a pilot writing program designed to help them to develop their writing and explore their interests by sharing their writing with a real audience. Students will be using personal weblogs to post their writing to the internet.

A weblog, or blog as they are commonly called, is a special type of web page that can be created and easily updated using a web browser. Each new entry has its own date stamp. Each entry has a comments section where visitors to the blog may leave comments for the author.

How it Works

Each week Ms. Tammy will teach a writing lesson using the 6-Trait writing model. After the lesson, students will write an entry for their blog. They may choose the topic, but they need to make use of the skills taught in the lesson to help to craft their writing. The emphasis is on the quality, not the quantity of what they write. When students are done polishing their writing, they have it reviewed by a teacher before it is published to the web.

Students will have two extra computer sessions most weeks to provide them with the time needed to complete their weekly blogging assignment. Students may also work from home. All that is required is an internet connection and a web browser. Students are able to save their work as drafts before publishing it to their blog. Directions for working from home will be provided.

Having a real audience is one of the key components to this program. In addition to receiving comments from their classmates, Ms. Tammy's students will receive comments from other fourth and fifth grade classes who visit their blogs. We are arranging for students in other parts of the world visit our blogs and comment on the writing. Parents are also invited to visit the blogs and respond to the writing. Potentially, anyone on the internet could respond to our blogs, however, it is not likely that the world at large will stumble across them.

Security

This blogging project is designed to minimize risk to your child. The only personally identifying information included in the blog will be their first name. There will be no mention of our school name or our location. Students are allowed to post their interests and opinions, but not their age, e-mail address, photographs of themselves, or other sensitive information.

Assessment

The weekly blog assignments will be part of your child's language arts grade this term. As with other projects they have completed this year, students will receive a scoring rubric that explains the expectations for these assignments. The rubric will include a section for the comments they leave in other students' blogs.

Resources

– Blogs created by fifth grade students in the USA

http://itc.blogs.com/marcos/

– BBC News article about blogging in a school in the UK

http://news.bbc.co.uk/1/hi/magazine/3804773.stm

Permission

Before your child may start posting to their blog, we are asking for you and your child to discuss and sign the following form. Please return the form to Ms. Tammy.

Blogging Terms and Conditions

1. Students using blogs are expected to act safely by keeping personal information out of their posts. You agree to not post or give out your family name, password, user name, e-mail address, home address, school name, city, country or other information that could help someone locate or contact you in person. You may share your interests, ideas, and preferences.

2. Students using blogs agree to not share their user name or password with anyone besides their teachers and parents. You agree to never log in as another student.

3. Students using blogs are expected to treat blogspaces as classroom spaces. Speech that is inappropriate for class is not appropriate

for your blog. While we encourage you to engage in debate and conversation with other bloggers, we also expect that you will conduct yourself in a manner reflective of a representative of this school.

4. Student blogs are to be a forum for student expression. However, they are first and foremost a tool for learning, and as such will sometimes be constrained by the various requirements and rules of classroom teachers. Students are welcome to post on any school-appropriate subject.

5. Students blogs are to be a vehicle for sharing student writing with real audiences. Most visitors to your blog who leave comments will leave respectful, helpful messages. If you receive a comment that makes you feel uncomfortable or is not respectful, tell your teacher right away. Do not respond to the comment.

6. Students using blogs take good care of the computers by not downloading or installing any software without permission, and not clicking on ads or competitions.

7. Students who do not abide by these terms and conditions may lose their opportunity to take part in this project.

I have read and understood these blogging terms and conditions.
I agree to uphold them.

Student's signature: _____ Date: _____

Parent's signature: _____ Date: _____

Used with permission of Susan Sedro.

SUMMARY

- The Web has changed from a "read only" resource to a "read AND write" tool where we can all contribute ideas and products.
- Journalism, politics, and business are being transformed by this new Web.
- Tools like Weblogs, wikis, RSS, social bookmarks, podcasting, and others have the potential to transform education as well.
- Although publishing student work to the Web is seen as risky by some, it can be done in ways that balance the power of publishing for an audience with the need to keep our students safe.

2 Weblogs: Pedagogy and Practice

The first time I saw a Weblog, I knew I was looking at something very different from a "regular" Webpage. Metafilter.org was one of only a handful of collaborative/community blogs back in 2001, where thousands of "members" were able to post funny or interesting links to a page, and where other members could leave their own opinions about those links just as easily. It was, and is, a fairly undistinguished looking site; lots of text and very few of the typical bells and whistles. But I will never forget the first time I posted my opinion, and the first time someone responded to it. There was something really powerful about *easily* being able to share resources and ideas with a Web *audience* that was willing to share back what they thought about those ideas.

In essence, that's still what I find so powerful about Weblogs today, more than four years later. Writing to the Web is easy. And there is an audience for my ideas. Those two concepts are at the core of why I think Weblogs have such huge potential in an educational setting.

What exactly is a Weblog? In its most general sense, a Weblog is an easily created, easily updateable Website that allows an author (or authors) to publish instantly to the Internet from any Internet connection. The earliest blogs were literally "Web logs" or lists of sites a particular author visited on any given day that would be revised by changing the HTML code and updating the file on a server. But soon, the Internet geeks who maintained these sites developed software to automate the process and allow other people to collaborate. Happily, blogging today doesn't require any knowledge of code or FTP. It takes as much skill as sending an e-mail.

Figure 2.1   Technology Educator Tim Wilson's Weblog has a typical look and feel with daily content added in the middle column and links added to the right. (Used with permission of Tim Wilson.)

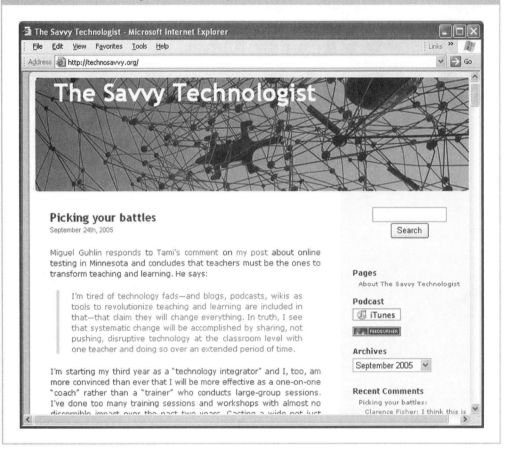

But what really distinguishes a blog from your run-of-the-mill Website is much more than process; it's what you'll find there. Weblogs are not built on static chunks of content. Instead, they are comprised of reflections and conversations that in many cases are updated every day (if not three or four times a day). Blogs engage readers with ideas and questions and links. They ask readers to think and to respond. They demand interaction.

Take teacher and blogger Tim Wilson's "The Savvy Technologist" blog as an example (http://technosavvy.org/, as shown in Figure 2.1). Visitors to his site can see his latest post at the top of the middle column, and if they scroll down the page, they can read what Tim has been posting for the last couple of months. Among the things readers might find are reflections from his daily work, links to interesting or educational sites on the Web, ideas for lessons, or responses to the thoughts and ideas of other bloggers. And for every post, readers can leave a comment that subsequent visitors to the site will be able to view. Typical comments on Tim's blog come from other teachers who share their own experiences, ask questions for clarification or to push his thinking, and offer links to other relevant pieces of content. In this way, blogs are a collaborative space, as readers become a part of the writing and learning process.

Tim's Weblog is also filled with links, another key characteristic of Weblogs. He has links to podcasts that he's created, personal affiliations, and a long list of other bloggers whom he reads regularly. Just about every post in his blog has a link in it which is just a part of good blog practice. (Being able to connect ideas and resources via linking is one of Weblogging's most important strengths.) And every post is itself a link so that others who read Tim's ideas can write about them on their own blogs and send their own readers Tim's way. That, in fact, is one of the key ways that community among bloggers is built.

But make no mistake, Tim's Weblog is every bit a Website. He can include graphics, photos, video, and audio files; his blog can have almost any feature a more traditional Website can have. Some of this depends upon the Weblog software and the skill level of the user, but for the most part, there isn't much that you can't do. And the best part is that most "blogwares" now come with a pretty impressive list of professional looking templates right out the box, so even though Tim may have personalized the look of his site somewhat, there's no start-up design even necessary.

Or take "Meredith's Page!" which was the name of the Weblog used by one of my former journalism students (http://central.hcrhs .k12.nj.us/mf069/). Readers of her site will find reflections on the work she did in class, homework assignments handed in through the Weblog, and links to articles that she has found relevant or interesting to her studies. She also has a running news feed from Google news about the topic she was writing her story about, teen apathy. In this way, she can easily check her blog to see if there are any new angles to her story. Readers will also find comments from classmates, teachers, and from Scott Higham, the Pulitzer Prize–winning journalist from the *Washington Post* who mentored her through her article process. Ultimately, Meredith's Weblog became her online archive of all the work related to our class.

In large measure, it is blogs that have opened up the Read/Write frontier for content creation to the Web, and millions of people have been quick to take advantage of the opportunity. Remember, a new blog is being created every second, and that shows no signs of slowing down. Now that doesn't mean that everyone who creates a blog becomes a dedicated blogger; two-thirds of all blogs go for more than two months without being updated. But it does mean that instant Web publishing for the masses is here. What those masses decide to do with it is another question. There are blogs about dogs and frogs, even people who wear clogs. There are flying blogs and frying blogs, crying blogs, and dying blogs. There are blogs for every age (my six-year-old son Tucker blogs), every occupation, every nationality, every . . . well, you get the idea. Blogs are hot.

But just to be clear, there are, I think, variations on the blogging theme that are important to identify. Millions of young adults have created sites at Weblog hosting services like Live Journal, Myspace.com, and Xanga.com, and by and large these authors are said to be bloggers. It's encouraging, to say the least, that so many of our would-be students have embraced the concept of publishing to the Web, and it bodes well for our use of these technologies in the classroom. What's somewhat discouraging, to me at least, is that these teenagers use these sites more as social tools than learning tools, and that their behavior is sometimes reckless. In the spring and summer of 2005, there was a rash of stories heralding the dangers of blogs as resources for predators, and about teenagers divulging too much of themselves (in text and photo) online. Although that is definitely cause for concern and action, my fear is that the powerful instructional uses of the tool are being at best ignored and at worst not even being considered. I would argue that what most adolescents are doing at these sites is more journaling than blogging, and from a classroom viewpoint, it's an important distinction to make. As I'll show a bit later, blogging is a genre that engages students and adults in a process of thinking in words, not simply an accounting of the days events or feelings. In fact, learning specialists Fernette and Brock Eide's research shows that blogging in its truest form has a great deal of potential positive impact on students. They found that blogs can

- Promote critical and analytical thinking
- Be a powerful promoter of creative, intuitive, and associational thinking
- Promote analogical thinking
- Be a powerful medium for increasing access and exposure to quality information
- Combine the best of solitary reflection and social interaction (Eide Neurolearning Blog, 2005)

More about that later.

WEBLOGS IN SCHOOLS

The early adopters of Weblogs in the classroom have already created a wide variety of ways to use them, and they have shown that blogs can enhance and deepen learning. Even at this still-early stage of development, blogs are being used as class portals, online filing cabinets for student work, e-portfolios, collaborative space, knowledge management, and even school Websites. Through the unique process of blogging, which will be discussed in much more detail in a moment, students are learning to read more critically, think about that reading more analytically, and write more clearly. And, they are building relationships with peers, teachers, mentors, and professionals within the Weblog environment.

If you're wondering just how flexible a Weblog can be as a teaching tool, see the lengthy list of uses at the end of this chapter created by Anne Davis, an elementary school teacher and Weblog advocate in Conyers, Georgia. And with a little thought and experimentation, I'm sure we could add plenty more ideas as well. In the meantime, here's a closer look at how educators have been using Weblogs in their schools.

Class Portal

One trend that shows no sign of stopping is the movement of curriculum to a digital, online environment. Although some schools invest in expensive content management systems like Blackboard, many Weblog packages can accomplish almost as much at a much lesser cost. In this vein, a great entry point for Weblog use is to build a class portal to communicate information about the class and to archive course materials. From a teaching standpoint, having a place to publish the course curriculum, syllabus, class rules, homework assignments, rubrics, handouts, and presentations makes a Weblog a powerful course management tool. When I created a portal for my journalism classes (see Figure 2.2), I was amazed at how frequently my students started using it and at how much time I saved by not having to dig out duplicate copies of things that I had already handed out. Further, it drastically reduced the frequency of the "I didn't know we had homework" or "That was due today?" responses when my students didn't do their work. I'd just simply say, "It was on the blog."

For the most part, parents love the transparency and the ability to access class materials. The Weblog software that I used, Manila (http://manila.userland.com) had a feature that allowed me to create a personal listserv that would automatically generate an e-mail every

Figure 2.2 My journalism class Weblog served as the daily meeting place for my students and featured links to homework, notes, and discussions.

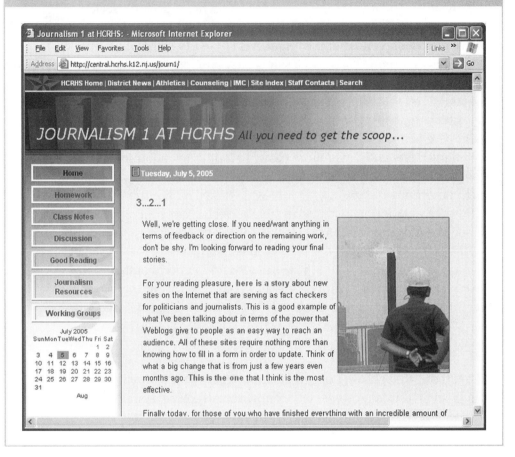

time I posted to the blog. So, I sent home a note to parents asking if they wanted to join, and in no time I had 15 parents who were receiving instant notification any time a new homework assignment or class handout was posted. (I could also do this via RSS, which we'll discuss in Chapter 5.)

The class portal Weblog makes it easy to communicate with peers who might be teaching the same course. I know my department chair liked the ability to visit the blog to see what we were up to and to get any information she might need about the class. Portals are a great way to get comfortable with the transparency that Weblogs provide.

Online Filing Cabinet

Giving students their own Weblogs can change much about the traditional classroom. Coupled with a classroom portal space, there's a good chance the class can go paperless as students simply post their work online for peer and teacher response. This creates a digital filing cabinet for students to archive their work and, in effect, creates a space for an online portfolio of work. This has a number of obvious advantages.

First, students never misplace their work. The dog never eats it; it's either in their blog or not. From a simple keeping track of papers perspective, this can make life much easier for teachers. If questions arise about whether or not a student handed in homework, the teacher can just look in the student's Weblog. (Some blogs even have time stamps on posts, so teachers can really enforce strict deadlines.)

Second, having all of their work organized in one place makes for some great opportunity for student reflection. It's very easy for students to look back over their work and, hopefully, see the growth they've accomplished. This is also true if peer, teacher, or mentor give feedback and respond in the blog. And remember that Weblogs are searchable; if a student is looking for a particular assignment or post, it's usually not too hard to locate it.

Finally, work on a Weblog can be shared with others who might be interested or invested in the student's progress. Just like with a classroom portal site, it's easy for parents to follow along as a student posts his or her work. This holds true for counselors, mentors, and peers as well. It's that transparency thing again.

Now think for a moment if students had Weblogs set up from the time they started school to the time they graduated. What they could have at the end would be a comprehensive history of their work and learning that was searchable and shareable, one that would provide a great resource for reflection or future study. And it would be an artifact that students could use to show expertise in a particular vocation or to impress potential college admissions officers. Either way, having that record of learning would be a very useful thing.

E-Portfolio

It's not a huge leap to jump from blog filing cabinet to blog portfolio. The traditional portfolio process is supported almost perfectly by Weblogs. First, students collect the work they might want to consider highlighting in their portfolio and then they select those that represent their best work. They then reflect on the choices they made, something they can easily do in a blog post. Finally, they publish the result for others to see. Even more powerful is the idea that these portfolios could conceivably span many grades and many classes.

In fact, E-portfolio guru Helen Barrett created online portfolios using more than 15 different software packages, many of them Weblogs (Barrett, 2004).

Collaborative Space

One of the biggest potentials of Weblogs is the ability to create spaces where students can collaborate with others online. Although collaborative learning has been a buzzword in American education for some time now, the Read/Write Web opens up all sorts of new possibilities for students to learn from each other or from authors or scientists or other professionals who can now work side by side in digital space even though they may be far away from one another physically.

It was a collaboration between my junior and senior students and Sue Monk Kidd, the author of the best-selling *The Secret Life of Bees* (Kidd, 2002), that really sold me on the potential and power of Weblogs as a learning tool (see Figure 2.3). Our school adopted the book into the curriculum just 9 months after it had been released, and because it was so new, I thought to use a Weblog to have my students create an online reader's guide to the book. In the process, I contacted the book's publicist to see if the author might want to join us in our study of the book. Much to my delight, after a few back-and-forth e-mails explaining what a Weblog was and how it worked, she agreed. So, while my students read and commented online, Sue Monk Kidd was able to follow along and then respond to a series of questions they had at the end of the book. Her 2,300-word response really floored us all. It started this way:

Dear Students,

It is an exceptionally nice honor to have you reading my novel in your Modern American Literature class! I'm extremely impressed with your weblog, which I've been following. What fun for the author to listen in on your discussions and see the wonderful and provocative artistic interpretations that you've created. The experience has opened my eyes to new ideas about my own work! (*The Secret Life of Bees: Questions for the author,* 2002)

She went on to describe how the characters were formed, where the symbols came from, and how she came to write many of the important scenes in the book. These were insights that no one but my students were able to benefit from (and anyone else who had stumbled onto the blog!)

Figure 2.3   My class studied the *Secret Life of Bees* in a Weblog and collaborated with each other and the author of the book, Sue Monk Kidd.

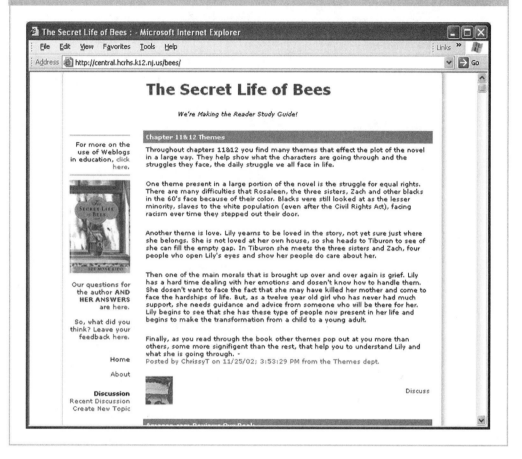

Since then, our students have collaborated with Pulitzer Prize–winning journalists, elementary school kids in Georgia, high school students in Poland, theater troupes in Oklahoma, and the list goes on. We've shared text, pictures, audio, and video, and we've engaged in some real learning from each other. In short, the blog has allowed us to build a community around our collaborations, and it has enhanced the depth of our curriculum.

Knowledge Management and Articulation

Not every use of Weblogs in schools has to involve students. In fact, blogs are a great way of communicating internally as well. School committees and groups that meet on a regular basis can use a blog to archive minutes of meetings, continue dialogues between get-togethers, share links to relevant information, and store documents and presentations for easy access later on. They are a great way to manage and communicate the knowledge that gets created.

In addition, districts can use Weblogs as articulation tools to highlight and share best practices, lesson plans, and "learning objects" such as worksheets or projects. Teachers no longer have to be in the same room to discuss what is and isn't working in their classrooms.

School Website

Finally, Weblogs can be used as a building block for a school Website. A major complaint about school Websites is that few of them are updated on a regular basis. That's an easy fix with a Weblog site. Imagine if each department had its own blog that it could maintain as needed. Imagine if all the clubs and activities, all the sports teams, and all the student government bodies had their own site that they could update. The overall school site would move from a static, wait-for-the-Webmaster-to-update-it type site to a dynamic every-day-there's-something-new type site.

Take a look at the Meriwether-Lewis Elementary School site, for instance (lewiselementary.org; see Figure 2.4). Principal Tim Lauer, who is an ed-blogging pioneer in his own right at his blog Educational/Technology (http://tim.lauer.name/), has used Weblogs to increase communication with parents and staff, post pictures and student work, keep the yearly calendar, and really create a community around the site. Teachers post weekly "Classroom Notes" that serve as a running diary of what students are doing and achieving.

Now that's not to say that everyone should be given carte blanche to post whatever they think is interesting. It's a good idea to designate a site "master" for each blog who reviews content before it gets published. And it's also a good idea to have at least one person who sees everything that goes up. (This is easier than it sounds with RSS, as I'll discuss in Chapter 5.) But there is no doubt that students, teachers, parents, and community members will all be better served by having up-to-date, relevant information at their fingertips through a Weblog or Website.

This is by no means the definitive list of how to use blogs. In fact, educators are using them in many creative ways, from creating a portal to the school library to using them as a collaborative reflection space for new teachers and their mentors, to professional development sites for staff. As Anne Davis likes to say, "The possibilities are endless!"

Figure 2.4   Principal Tim Lauer uses a Weblog as his school Website. (Meriwether Lewis Elementary School, Portland, Oregon. Used with permission.)

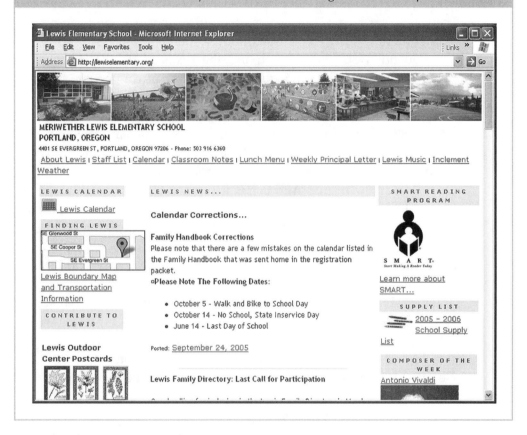

THE PEDAGOGY OF WEBLOGS

So what exactly can Weblogs do to improve student learning? Why should classroom teachers consider blogs as a tool to deliver their curriculum? Because the Read/Write Web is still in its relative infancy, the answers to these questions are just now beginning to be clarified. But there are some basic aspects of blogs that make them an attractive addition to the teacher's toolbox nonetheless.

First, Weblogs are truly a constructivist tool for learning. Because the content that students and teachers create is on the World Wide Web, it is content that becomes a part of the wider body of knowledge that the Internet represents. It is searchable; people can find it and use it. *The Secret Life of Bees* Weblog that my students created has been accessed more than 1.5 million times as of this writing. Needless to say, not all of those people came from our school.

That potential audience is one of the most important aspects of the Read/Write Web. The idea that the relevance of student work no longer ends at the classroom door can not only be a powerful motivator but can also create a significant shift in the way we think about the assignments and work we ask of our students in the first place.

Second, Weblogs truly expand the walls of the classroom. The Internet has always provided the possibility of connecting students with others outside the classroom via e-mail and chat groups. But now that collaboration can be much more accessible and much more diverse. We can create sites where classes from disparate geographies can conduct all sorts of experiments; share the results through text; picture, audio, or video; and invite expert scientists into the process to reflect on the results. And in a world that is moving more and more toward a business model of the collaborative construction of content, learning to work with far-flung collaborators is becoming an important literacy.

Third, blogs archive the learning that teachers and students do, facilitating all sorts of reflection and metacognitive analysis that was previously much more cumbersome. From an organizational standpoint, the ability to keep histories of work in an organized, searchable, easily shareable space is an important development.

Fourth, the Weblog is a democratic tool that supports different learning styles. For those students who might be more reticent in class, a blog gives them the opportunity to share in writing the ideas they may be too shy to speak. Everyone has a voice in the conversation, and all ideas, even the instructor's, are given equal presentation in the blog. As students participate, they also take ownership of the space, and depending on how teachers frame that participation, this can lead to a greater sense of participation.

Fifth, the use of Weblogs can enhance the development of expertise in a particular subject. Students who blog in educational settings usually focus their reading and writing on one topic, which helps bring about topic-specific expertise. A student who uses a blog to track stories and reflections on the genocide in Darfur, for example, is creating a database of learning that she can continue to build on.

Finally, blogs can teach students the new literacies they will need to function in an ever expanding information society. The extent of our collective knowledge doubles every 18 months (Olofson, 1999), and as more and more information comes online, it's imperative that we give our students the skills to analyze and manage it. The act of writing in a Weblog, or "blogging," can go a long way to teaching skills such as research, organization, and synthesis of ideas.

In fact, research on the effects of Weblogs on K–12 students is still in its infancy. But the anecdotal results reported by many of the educator bloggers discussed here give broad outlines to a picture that will no doubt soon come into focus. In general, students at all levels show more interest in their work, and their ability to locate and reflect upon their work is greatly enhanced, as are the opportunities for collaborative learning.

A New Writing Genre

Posting to a Weblog can take many forms. Students can write about personal reactions to topics covered in class, post links, write reflectively, and summarize or annotate reading. They can use blogs as journals or as places to publish creative writing for larger audiences. The possibilities really are endless. But by their very structure, blogs facilitate what I think is a new form of genre that could be called "connective writing," a form that forces those who do it to read carefully and critically, that demands clarity and cogency in its construction, that is done for a wide audience, and that links to the sources of the ideas expressed.

Before getting further into this discussion, let's take a look at a sample of this type of writing from a student in journalism teacher Tom McHale's class. Tom, who teaches at my school, has his students use their blogs to become experts in an area of their choice, and in this example, his student Rachel is blogging about self-image:

> A recent trend has started a shift from society's focus on the face to the hands (http://www.nytimes.com/2005/06/02/fashion/thursdaystyles/02skin.html?8dpc&oref=login). People are opening up a new front in the war against aging by paying particular attention to the maintenance of their hands.
>
> When I first read this article, I could not believe the words that I was reading. But almost immediately after finishing, I began wondering if my peer sitting next to me was just watching me type or actually analyzing the physical state of my hands. Sure, people interact physically each day whether they are greeting friends or waving "hi" down the hallway, but how does the person receiving these gestures really feel? Do my friends honestly judge me by the softness, or lack thereof, of my hands each day?
>
> After considering this for a while, I finally hit a road block and recognized my own stupidity. I was falling into the

materialistic trap of our own society. People are becoming too concerned with having the best clothing and the perfect hairdo each day. Society's obsession with plastic surgery (http://www.joshgreene.com/surgery/) to correct problems that no one would probably have ever noticed has gone too far. Sure, I may hesitate to shake a hand with unclean, fungi-infested nails, but I'd hesitate more if I had found out that they had spent thousands of dollars on plastic surgery to make the veins on the back of their hands less visible.

This new obsession with spending money on creams and serums (http://query.nytimes.com/gst/abstract.html?res= F1081FF7395D0C718EDDAF0894DC404482&fta=y&incamp= archive:article_related%22) promising smooth, appealing hands is just weird. No one in their right mind spends time making sure that their friends' fingers are flawless. I can't even think of a time when a person's hands even had an effect on me. It seems useless for someone to go out to a hand spa and waste hours receiving "hand masks" that promise to eliminate dead skin and wrinkles. And if this is a matter of showing off what you can afford, then I feel sorry for these hand-a-phobics. It would look a lot cooler to me if someone spent this extra money to help out others rather than spending on the appearance of his own hands. Last time I checked, I wasn't able to tell the difference between a hand that had received a paraffin wax treatment and one that hadn't.

Still, Americans have spent a whooping $7 billion on nail treatments in 2004. It's understandable that someone wants to spend five dollars on a simple lotion to prevent dry skin, but not if he turns to his local plastic surgeon for a hand lift. I don't understand what a person could possibly get out of this besides a hard time writing in the days following the proce-dure. What problems can we possibly rely on plastic surgery to solve next? I'm not so sure, but I did notice a little dis-coloration on my belly button. (http://central.hcrhs.k12.nj.us/ rv211/2005/06/02#a57; retrieved on May 23, 2005.)

As that example shows, connective writing is, for the most part, expository writing, but the process starts with reading. Remember the origin of the Weblog? It was a list of the sites that someone had visited and, presumably, read. But more than just reading, bloggers that write in this way learn to read critically because as they read, they look for important ideas to write about. It's an important first step, for as Samuel Johnson said, "I hate to read a writer who has written more than he has read."

This, in turn, requires critical thinking skills as they consider their audience and clarify the purpose of the writing. Many times, one post is the synthesis of the reading of many texts, so bloggers must be able to find connections and articulate the relevance of those connections. In composing the post, this genre of writing demands organization and clarity as well as a keen awareness of audience. Also expected is the writer's own reflections on or experience with the ideas she's writing about.

Throughout this process, bloggers are constantly making editorial decisions, and these decisions are more complex than those made when writing for a limited audience. Because students are regularly selecting content to include or link to, they learn to find and identify accurate and trustworthy sources of information. Because of a potential audience that goes beyond the classroom, they pay more attention to the editorial correctness of the post as well.

Although it may seem that the final step in the process is to finally publish the post to the Weblog, this connective writing genre actually continues post publication. That's because of the ability of readers to interact with the post, another example of the connective aspect of it. This is a crucial distinction that necessarily changes the purpose of the writing. When I post to my Weblog, I anticipate the reader's response as much as I can, but ultimately, my post is still a draft, a way to test my best ideas and writing against an audience. When readers do respond or give feedback, blogging continues. In fact, some would argue that a true blog post is never really finished, that as long as it's out there for others to interact with, the potential for deeper insight exists. Konrad Glogowski, a fourth-grade teacher from Ontario, says that his students see this type of blogging "as transactional writing, as writing to be interacted with, to be returned to and reflected upon" (Glogowski, 2005). In fact, comments are a powerful motivator of student writing in blogs, especially when those comments come from sources outside of the classroom walls.

The differences between blogging in this manner and writing as we traditionally think of it are clear: Writing stops; blogging continues. Writing is inside; blogging is outside. Writing is monologue; blogging is conversation. Writing is thesis; blogging is synthesis . . . none of which minimizes the importance of writing. But writing becomes an ongoing process, one that is not just done for the contrived purposes of the classroom. Ken Smith, a writing instructor at Indiana University, puts it this way:

Instead of assigning students to go write, we should assign them to go read and then link to what interests them and write about why it does and what it means, not in order to make a connection or build social capital but because it is through quality linking . . . that one first comes in contact with the essential acts of blogging: close reading and interpretation. Blogging, at base, is writing down what you think when you read others. If you keep at it, others will eventually write down what they think when they read you, and you'll enter a new realm of blogging, a new realm of human connection. (Smith, 2004)

That's a pretty powerful vision of what blogging can be.

Doing connective writing in blogs, then, is a different experience than just posting. If we take a look at the spectrum of different types of Weblog posts, we can start to see where posting ends and blogging as an academic exercise begins:

1. Posting assignments. (Not blogging)

2. Journaling, i.e. "This is what I did today." (Not blogging)

3. Posting links. (Not blogging)

4. Links with descriptive annotation, i.e., "This site is about . . . ." (Not really blogging either, but getting close depending on the depth of the description)

5. Links with analysis that gets into the meaning of the content being linked. (A simple form of blogging)

6. Reflective, metacognitive writing on practice without links. (Complex writing, but simple blogging, I think. Commenting would probably fall in here somewhere.)

7. Links with analysis and synthesis that articulate a deeper understanding or relationship to the content being linked and written with potential audience response in mind. (Real blogging)

8. Extended analysis and synthesis over a longer period of time that builds on previous posts, links, and comments. (Complex blogging)

A quick look at the "Standards for the Language Arts" written by the National Council of Teachers of English also suggests the potential of Weblogs as a classroom tool (see the end of this chapter). In almost every one of the 12 standards, blogs have obvious relevance, whether it's that "Students employ a wide range of strategies as they write and use different writing process elements appropriately to communicate with different audiences for a variety of purposes," something bloggers do by the very nature of their process, or "Students participate as knowledgeable, reflective, creative, and critical members of a variety of literacy communities." Blogs create and connect these communities like few other tools.

Scaffolding Blogging

How then to introduce this new genre to students? When is an appropriate age to begin teaching our students the skills that blogging encompasses? Certainly, elementary students could not be expected to do the consistent analytical thinking and writing that extended blogging requires. But to start, we could provide or ask students to find interesting and relevant sites of information and teach them how to write about what they find useful at those sites. We could ask them to do some basic deconstruction of the design of the site, or we could ask them to write about what more they would like to see. Even at this level, teachers may consider recruiting an audience to interact with students, allowing them to begin exploring what it means to write with an ear for readership and to enter into conversations about ideas. And it's never too early to start thinking about bringing primary sources like authors, scientists, politicians, and the like into the classroom through the blog so students can ask questions and reflect on the answers. But there's also nothing wrong with asking other teachers or friends or even parents to become a part of the learning as well.

Middle school students might be asked to work at becoming "experts" about topics that they care about by using blogs. They might be ready to compare information from different sources and to reflect on their process of determining what sources are trustworthy and which are not. Again, structuring ways to include reader response is an important ingredient in helping to develop blogging skills.

Older students can be asked to begin using Weblogs for extended study and reflection on a topic. They could be asked to reflect and build on previous ideas, incorporate the feedback from readers, synthesize reading from a number of different sources, and advance new ideas or interpretations of the topic.

This is just one way to think about the introduction of blogging as a viable and valuable writing genre in the classroom. The thousands of educators who are now entering the blogosphere will certainly provide us with many more creative examples in years to come.

BLOGGING ACROSS THE CURRICULUM

Although the nature of Weblogs makes them fairly obvious tools for teaching writing and reading, educators are using blogs in all areas of the curriculum to collaborate with subject-specific experts, to archive learning, to share results of experiments, and to publish student work. Blogging across the curriculum offers students and teachers not only the ability to infuse writing into all disciplines, it facilitates connections in ways that plain paper cannot. Students can work on math problems with peers from other classes. Science experiments can be run concurrently at any number of different sites across the country or around the world with student researchers comparing and reflecting on the results on a Weblog. Language students can create conversations with native speakers, phys ed students can log and analyze their workouts or diets, and history students can construct resource sites for their study of ancient civilizations and conflicts.

Here are a few specific examples of teachers employing Weblogs with their students.

Pre-Cal 40S (http://pc40s.blogspot.com/)

Darren Kuropatwa (2005) is a math teacher from Winnipeg who in the spring of 2005 used his Weblog as a starting point for the introduction of new concepts, a place to share links and ideas with his students, and a forum for discussion about the class (see Figure 2.5). The subtitle of the site says it all: "An interactive log for students and parents in my Pre-Cal 40S class. This ongoing dialogue is as rich as YOU make it. Visit often and post your comments freely." Darren uses Blogger software and allows his students to post to the class blog by making them all team members. (More on that in the next chapter.) He keeps his own blog at http://adifference.blogspot.com/ where he reflects on his teaching and his use of blogs. In his first post there, he writes: "The breakneck evolution of technologies on the internet is changing they way we teach. It's hard to keep up. I hope to use this blog to record and reflect on my personal evolution of how to integrate these technologies into my teaching."

His Pre-Cal 40S site has the feel of an online neighborhood where he and his students post pictures of pi-shaped structures,

Figure 2.5 Darren Kuropatwa's site is a good example of how disciplines like math and science can use blogs. (Used with permission of Darren Kuropatwa.)

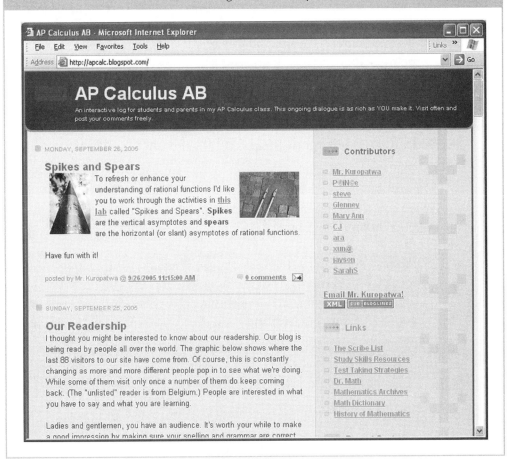

reflect on how to study for tests, and share what they're learning. One pretty typical post by a student highlights an "a-ha" moment she experienced:

> Let me just say that Mr. K doesn't put these links to be stared at. It was written to serve its purpose of helping us to learn and improve our studies. Personally I found out that it's easier for me to learn from the online quizzes than from the assignments. (Kuropatwa, 2005)

Interestingly, in the 2005–06 school year, Derek plans to expand his use of blogs to all six of his classes instead of just one.

I'm also working to encourage greater collaboration between teachers teaching the same course (we'll share responsibility for overseeing the blogs of courses we have in common) and to build in a mentorship program where former students of earlier blogs mentor new students of current blogs. This year will be my experiment in increased collaboration and mentorship; the blog is here to stay. (Kuroptawa, personal communication, August 30, 2005)

Bud's Blog Experiment (http://budtheteacher.blogspot.com/)

The title of Bud Hunt's Weblog site says it all. It's all about the journey that he and his students took to implement blogs in their classroom. It gives a great introduction to what it is that makes Weblogs potentially powerful tools:

> We're very mindful as we begin this learning experience together that other students and teachers might be reading what we're writing, so we're thinking very carefully about our audiences and our writing as we compose. Oh yeah—we're also laughing and having a great time! (Hunt, 2005)

Bud teaches at an alternative high school in Longmont, Colorado. Like Darren, he writes reflectively about his practice and his learning. In fact, in his first post he says "I am beginning this blog because I am a teacher and I am in need of an education."

Bud created blogs for all of the students in his class where they, well, blog. They go through the process of reading and then writing about topics that are important to them, and Bud culls the most interesting or provocative posts on the class site. And that's an important role for the teacher in a Weblog community, to constantly be on the lookout for student posts that can inspire or teach and share them with everyone else in blog fashion.

The Write Weblog (http://itc.blogs.com/thewriteweblog/)

As previously noted, Anne Davis is one of the true pioneers of blogs in classrooms. Her Weblog "EduBlog Insights" (http://anne.teachesme.com/) is a great starting point for teachers wanting to see firsthand what happens when you mix blogs and students. The Write Weblog (http://itc.blogs.com/thewriteweblog/2004/11/who_says_elemen.html) is a place where fifth graders chronicled their learning

Figure 2.6   Anne Davis's "The Write Weblog" is a great example of how elementary school students can flourish using blogs. (Used with permission of Anne Davis.)

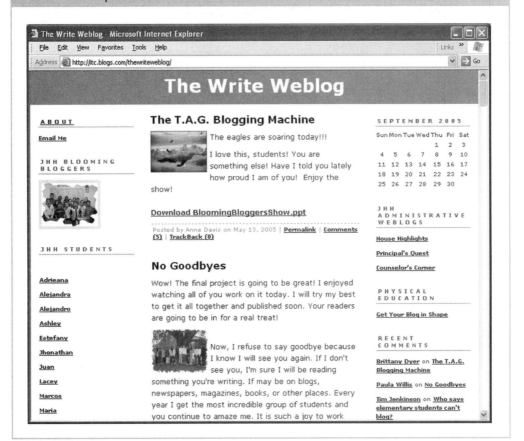

about writing and, from the looks of it, a lot of learning took place (see Figure 2.6). All students had their own blog where they reflected on their process and had conversations with readers, and their sites were open for anyone to read and comment on.

Like the others, Anne reflects often on her own learning through the use of Weblogs. A great example is a post called "Who Says Elementary Students Can't Blog?" in which after discussing her process for the day in some depth she writes: "This process of browsing, reading, learning, thinking and selecting topics will be the first order of the day for each session. I think this is going to work out well" (Davis, 2005).

The effect on the students in the class was profound. One girl, Paulina, wrote

One of the greatest things that happened to me was when I got chosen to have a blog. At first I thought it was just extra work, but then I started liking it. This has been a great year. We have learned so much and I hope that future generations will have a chance to experience what we have. (*Paulina's Club*, 2005. http://itc.blogs.com/paulina/2005/05/our_ lives_at_jh.html)

Depending on the focus, Weblogs in the classroom have the potential to affect student learning in many positive ways. Blogging can teach critical reading and writing skills, and it can lead to greater information management skills. It can help students become much more media and information literate by clarifying the choices they make about the content they write about, and it teaches them about how networks function, both human and computer, and it can teach the essential skill of collaboration.

BLOGS AS RESOURCES

But regardless of whether you and/or your students become bloggers, blogs have probably already become sources of information about whatever topics you might be studying. And this means that at the very least, you and your students will need to learn how to evaluate them for accuracy and trustworthiness. If anyone with an Internet connection can now get online and start blogging about any topic he or she wants, how do we know who to believe? The easy way is to not believe any of them since they are, at least in the traditional ways, unedited content. But that would be to ignore some very smart and relevant voices that are gaining more and more of a reputation as credible sources each day. And really, this is the work that is required of all of us if we are to be truly information literate in the twenty-first century.

Before getting to some specific strategies for determining valid sources, I would urge you to read long-time edblogger Stephen Downes's excellent post on the topic. Basically, Downes says, there is no way to tell for sure if something you read on the Web in general is true, and that we can no longer trust even traditional sources to always be accurate and tell the truth. In the end, "determining what to believe—or to not believe—is a matter of trust. You need to determine for yourself who to trust about what" (Downes, 2005).

I agree, and teachers and students have to realize that we've entered an age in which there are no longer many free passes when it comes to assessing the reliability of a source. As we've seen in the past few years, even the *New York Times* can get it horribly wrong, and if the 2004 presidential campaign cycle was any indication, it's getting easier and easier to say whatever you want in a book without any regard for truth or accuracy. (And that goes for both sides, by the way.)

So getting a handle on the reliability of Web content in general and blog content specifically takes time, much more than you or your students are used to. A first step is to try and find out as much as you can about the author of the Weblog. See if there is an "About" link that will lead to a name and some background on the author. What is her profession? What is her title? Where does her authority on the topic come from? You may want to do a name search on Google to see what comes up. Remember, though, that some bloggers prefer to stay anonymous, and although that obviously makes it difficult to use that person's ideas in research, it doesn't totally preclude it. Also, you might want to find out who owns a site by going to internic.com and doing a search for who registered the domain name.

Next, you may want to find out what kind of a reputation the blogger has among his peers. One way to do this is to go to the blog tracking site Technorati.com and enter the URL of the blog into the search form. The results will show you how many other bloggers have linked to that particular Weblog. In general, I would say that any site that has more than 100 links to it has earned a reputation as a good source of information by its community. But that doesn't mean that blogs with fewer links should be discounted, just as blogs with more than 100 should not be automatically accepted. Technorati is just a first step (blogger Tom Hoffman, 2005, has a great post on this topic at http://www.eschoolnews.com/eti/2005/06/000877.php). Students should be taught to take the time to evaluate the sites that are linking to a blog as well.

Also, take a look at the "blogroll" or list of blogs that the blogger links to. Again, try to find out as much as you can about the bloggers personal agenda, if there is one. Finally, take the time to read through some of the other posts on the site and click through to the links they include. Does the author's synthesis of what she is reading seem credible? Is there an obvious political bias or is something being sold? Are other people commenting and, if so, what are they saying?

You'll need to have these discussions with your students, many of whom will be apt to use the first source they find that supports their thesis. And you'll have to develop your own standards for blog sources. Ideally, for a blog to be used as a part of a research effort, you should be able to identify who the author is, what she does for a living, what her level of expertise is, and what judgments others have made about her. Anything less renders the source less than acceptable.

So, it's obvious that Weblogs are already making an impact on our curricula whether we are employing them as research tools or as publishing tools. These next few years promise to be very messy in terms of sorting through the issues of trust and reliability, but I can promise you this: becoming a blogger and blogging consistently is the absolute best way to navigate through the murkiness. There is no better way to understand the impact of the Read/Write Web than by becoming a part of it. And by the end of the next chapter, you'll be able to do just that.

CLASSROOM USES OF WEBLOGS

You might like to create a reflective, journal-type blog to . . .

- reflect on your teaching experiences.
- keep a log of teacher-training experiences.
- write a description of a specific teaching unit.
- describe what worked for you in the classroom or what didn't work.
- provide some teaching tips for other teachers.
- write about something you learned from another teacher.
- explain teaching insights you gain from what happens in your classes.
- share ideas for teaching activities or language games to use in the classroom.
- provide some how-to's on using specific technology in the class, describing how you used this technology in your own class.
- explore important teaching and learning issues.

You might like to start a class blog to . . .

- post class-related information such as calendars, events, homework assignments, and other pertinent class information.
- post assignments based on literature readings and have students respond on their own Weblogs, creating a kind of portfolio of their work.
- communicate with parents if you are teaching elementary school students.
- post prompts for writing.

- provide examples of classwork, vocabulary activities, or grammar games.
- provide online readings for your students to read and react to.
- gather and organize Internet resources for a specific course, providing links to appropriate sites and annotating the links as to what is relevant about them.
- post photos and comment on class activities.
- invite student comments or postings on issues in order to give them a writing voice.
- publish examples of good student writing done in class.
- showcase student art, poetry, and creative stories.
- create a dynamic teaching site, posting not only class-related information, but also activities, discussion topics, links to additional information about topics they are studying in class, and readings to inspire learning.
- create a literature circle (where groups of students read and discuss the same book).
- create an online book club.
- make use of the commenting feature to have students publish messages on topics being used to develop language skills.
- ask students to create their own individual course blogs, where they can post their own ideas, reactions, and written work.
- post tasks to carry out project-based learning tasks with students.
- build a class newsletter, using student-written articles and photos they take.
- link your class with another class somewhere else in the world.

You can encourage your students (either on your Weblog using the comments feature or on their own Weblogs) to blog . . .

- their reactions to thought-provoking questions.
- their reactions to photos you post.
- journal entries.
- results of surveys they carry out as part of a class unit.
- their ideas and opinions about topics discussed in class.

You can have your students create their own Weblogs to . . .

- learn how to blog.
- complete class writing assignments.
- create an ongoing portfolio of samples of their writing.
- express their opinions on topics you are studying in class.

- write comments, opinions, or questions on daily news items or issues of interest.
- discuss activities they did in class and tell what they think about them (You, the teacher, can learn a lot this way!).
- write about class topics, using newly learned vocabulary words and idioms.
- showcase their best writing pieces.

You can also ask your class to create a shared Weblog to . . .

- complete project work in small groups, assigning each group a different task.
- showcase products of project-based learning.
- complete a WebQuest (an online, structured research activity).

Share ideas you have for using Weblogs in education.
(http://anne.teachesme.com/2004/10/05)

STANDARDS FOR THE ENGLISH LANGUAGE ARTS SPONSORED BY NCTE AND IRA

The vision guiding these standards is that all students must have the opportunities and resources to develop the language skills they need to pursue life's goals and to participate fully as informed, productive members of society. These standards assume that literacy growth begins before children enter school as they experience and experiment with literacy activities—reading and writing, and associating spoken words with their graphic representations. Recognizing this fact, these standards encourage the development of curriculum and instruction that make productive use of the emerging literacy abilities that children bring to school. Furthermore, the standards provide ample room for the innovation and creativity essential to teaching and learning. They are not prescriptions for particular curriculum or instruction. Although we present these standards as a list, we want to emphasize that they are not distinct and separable; they are, in fact, interrelated and should be considered as a whole.

1. Students read a wide range of print and nonprint texts to build an understanding of texts, of themselves, and of the cultures of the United States and the world; to acquire new information; to

respond to the needs and demands of society and the workplace; and for personal fulfillment. Among these texts are fiction and nonfiction, classic and contemporary works.

2. Students read a wide range of literature from many periods in many genres to build an understanding of the many dimensions (e.g., philosophical, ethical, aesthetic) of human experience.

3. Students apply a wide range of strategies to comprehend, interpret, evaluate, and appreciate texts. They draw on their prior experience, their interactions with other readers and writers, their knowledge of word meaning and of other texts, their word identification strategies, and their understanding of textual features (e.g., sound–letter correspondence, sentence structure, context, graphics).

4. Students adjust their use of spoken, written, and visual language (e.g., conventions, style, vocabulary) to communicate effectively with a variety of audiences and for different purposes.

5. Students employ a wide range of strategies as they write and use different writing process elements appropriately to communicate with different audiences for a variety of purposes.

6. Students apply knowledge of language structure, language conventions (e.g., spelling and punctuation), media techniques, figurative language, and genre to create, critique, and discuss print and nonprint texts.

7. Students conduct research on issues and interests by generating ideas and questions and by posing problems. They gather, evaluate, and synthesize data from a variety of sources (e.g., print and nonprint texts, artifacts, people) to communicate their discoveries in ways that suit their purpose and audience.

8. Students use a variety of technological and information resources (e.g., libraries, databases, computer networks, video) to gather and synthesize information and to create and communicate knowledge.

9. Students develop an understanding of and respect for diversity in language use, patterns, and dialects across cultures, ethnic groups, geographic regions, and social roles.

10. Students whose first language is not English make use of their first language to develop competency in the English language arts and to develop understanding of content across the curriculum.

11. Students participate as knowledgeable, reflective, creative, and critical members of a variety of literacy communities.

12. Students use spoken, written, and visual language to accomplish their own purposes (e.g., for learning, enjoyment, persuasion, and the exchange of information).

(http://www.ncte.org/about/over/standards/110846.htm)

3 Weblogs: Get Started!

So if you believe as I do that Weblogs can play an important role in your classroom, then it's time to start thinking about the ways you can most effectively implement them for your own unique purposes.

The true potential of blogs in schools comes when students and teachers use them as publishing tools. And to me at least, the best way to fully understand the potential of Weblogs as a teaching and learning tool is to become a blogger. Just as writing teachers should write, and literature teachers should read, teachers who use blogs should, well, use blogs. Without question, the most profound learning experience of my life has been the ongoing education I have received by keeping my own Weblog for the past 4 years. The process of blogging and my use of the other tools that the Read/Write Web has spawned have not only made writing a daily part of my life, they have changed the way that I read and consume information.

Middlebury College professor Barbara Ganley, who uses Weblogs extensively in her courses, asks "How can a teacher expect her students to blog (or to use any other tool, strategy, or technique) if she doesn't use it herself, exploring the impact it has on her thinking, writing, research and creativity?" (Ganley, 2004b). She also says

> And as we all know, when a teacher believes in what she's doing and is confident in her tools, well, it rubs off on even the most resistant of students. As reflective research-teachers, we must continue to circle back and look at how what we do ties into our long-term educational goals." (Ganley, 2004a)

I agree. If we want our students to learn from blogs, we have to experience that learning firsthand or, as Ganley says, "get into their shoes."

Even more, I think teachers should blog to show students that it is something of value and to model appropriate ways of doing it. Remember, millions of kids are already blogging, so they certainly are enticed by the tool. But very few are using their sites as places of critical thinking and analytical writing and reflection. It's well and good to encourage and teach our students to blog, but they will surely give it up at the end of the semester unless we've shown them why it's important to keep writing and to keep learning. (No pressure.)

Getting started with blogging from a technical aspect is not difficult, and in a bit we'll talk about the easiest ways to begin. But from the perspective of writing for an audience and getting into the habit of regular reflection, it does take some effort to get the blog rolling, so to speak. The first step is to take some time to just read some good Weblogs. A good place to find some that might interest you is the "Find New Blogs" list at Bloglines.com (www.bloglines.com/topblogs), or you can look at the shortlist at the end of this chapter. (And don't forget the Edublogs Award site at http://incsub.org/awards/) Remember that reading Weblogs is a different type of reading than what you've previously done as well. Unlike books or newspaper and magazine articles, most blog posts are fairly short. There are links inviting you to investigate other sources. And most importantly, you can engage in a dialogue about the topic by reading the comments and, perhaps, leaving your own. In fact, posting on other people's blogs before you start your own is a great way to get the feel of publishing your thoughts. Just wait until that first person responds to something you've written; that's when you'll truly start to understand the power of the Read/Write Web.

START SMALL

When you're ready to begin your own blog, you might want to start small by using the first few posts to just create a link to something interesting that you've read along with a short excerpt, nothing more. You won't truly be "blogging" as described in the previous chapter yet, but you'll be getting a feel for the experience of publishing online, and you'll be scaffolding your blogging in similar ways to your students. When you get comfortable with the process, you may want to begin annotating the links you post with a couple of sentences that highlight what you think is meaningful or important about what you've read. As you get more settled into the rhythm of posting, begin to write more in depth about what you are reading, drawing on your own personal experiences and reflections. In this way, you'll come to understand the true mental work that is blogging. These types of posts should form the foundation of your blog work. That's not to say keeping a blog is all work and no play, however. Don't be afraid to include some posts that are totally personal or just for fun; your readers want to see the person behind the blog as well.

Another piece of advice: Be a public blogger. Put your name on your work, but make sure you understand the ramifications of doing so. Different schools have different comfort levels with teachers blogging, and I try to think very carefully about what I write about my own school in my blog. Remember, this is a learning tool and may not necessarily be the place where you want to air your complaints about the board of education, parents, or particular students. Public writing demands discretion, especially in an educational setting. And remember too that what you write stays with you. Each post contributes to your online portfolio that may turn up in future Google searches.

BLOGGING WITH STUDENTS

So, once you've become a blogger and you've decided to try Weblogs in your teaching practice, what's the best way to start? Obviously, before planning your blog work, you need to consider the level of Internet access that your students have both at school and at home. The good news is that more and more households are getting online, with more than 80% of households having Internet access at the end of 2004 and more coming online each day (Fox, 2005). The bad news is that until those numbers reach 100%, Weblogs will be out of reach for some teachers and students in this country. Although you can use blogs even if students don't have outside access to the Web, the possibilities for their use are much greater if they do.

Regardless of the level of connectivity, however, I would start small. The most obvious initial implementation is first to use Weblogs as a place to post homework assignments and relevant class links. Don't worry about collaborations or conversations at the outset. Just get used to how it feels to communicate information to your students online, and let your students get used to consuming that information in a different form. Let parents know that you've created a site for your class materials, and give them whatever information they need to get regular updates.

First, get students reading blogs. Prepare a list of Weblogs with appropriate content and look at some of those sites with your students. You may even want to show your own site. But because good blogging starts with good reading, it's important that you provide some models for them to look at and follow. With younger students, you may want to show what other elementary schools are doing, whereas with older students you may want to pick a few bloggers whom you've read and come to respect. Again, see the accompanying list for some suggestions.

Next, you may want to try letting students respond to the posts on your class blog. The first time I used Weblogs with one of my classes, I posted a question each day that I wanted them to think about and discuss after school. I asked them to make a certain number of responses to the questions during the week, and we modeled what the expectations were for those responses beforehand. I made sure the questions were sufficiently provocative, and most of my students went way beyond the required number of responses. It gave them a great opportunity to experience public writing in a safe way and to get the posting process down.

Having small groups of students actually start creating posts to the same Weblog is a great way to introduce them to blogging (in the "connective writing" sense) and to help them understand the process. Again, be very clear as to what your expectations are, and just as with any other writing genre, spend some time teaching them how to blog. Use your own blog as a model!

Finally, you may want to consider giving each student his or her own blog. But before you do, make sure you and your students are totally comfortable with the technology and with the concept of reading and working online. Although there's no doubt that more and more content will be created and consumed online in years to come, some have not yet done enough reading online to be totally comfortable with it. Giving each student a Weblog basically means a paperless classroom.

And giving them their own site invites a discussion of how much of that site should be their own. By that I mean can they add pictures and quotes of their liking, much as they might to their notebooks or lockers? Can they do journal-type writing that might be unrelated to the coursework? Can they write about their own passions regardless of whether or not those passions have any relevance to the curriculum? These types of questions might be negotiated with the students themselves. Although I believe that allowing students to personalize their spaces makes them more invested in their blogs, I also feel that it makes the assessment more difficult.

BLOG SAFETY

Regardless of how you start using Weblogs with students, make sure that students, parents, and even administrators are clear about the expectations and the reasoning behind it. And make sure everyone has the proper permissions. At our school, we made publishing to the Web a part of our Acceptable Use Policy that parents had to sign. I'd also encourage you to communicate to parents what safety precautions you have in place to protect student privacy. On the K–12 level, this may mean using only first names of students, or even pseudonyms for students with unique names. It means teaching kids never to publish personal identifiers about themselves or others. It means making sure they know the process for reporting problems in their blogs, whether technical or content related. It means doing professional development for staff that clarifies the uses and purposes of blogs. The more documentation and backup you have from students, parents, and administrators in terms of clarifying the use of the tool the better. Bud Hunt has a great resource for documents of these types at his "Blogging Policies and Resources Wiki" (http://www.budtheteacher.com/wiki/). And safety also means having in place a way to consistently monitor the activity on whatever blogs your students are using. I'll show you an easy way to do that in the chapter about RSS (Chapter 5).

When overseeing student blogs, the teachers' role becomes that of connector, not just evaluator. As you read what students write, try to respond by commenting back when appropriate. And link to the best student posts and ideas in the class blog. This is a very important habit to form. When you celebrate good work, or use students' unique ideas to drive further discussion, it goes a long way to creating a community of learners. Anne Davis is great at doing this, as her post titled "Tips from TheWriteTeam" shows: "Your posts today were excellent! I just had to pull one from each of you to share on our class blog. Here goes!" (Davis, 2005) She goes on to expertly weave together excerpts from all of her student blogs so they can easily see the things their peers are writing about and so feel that sense of accomplishment that Anne so wonderfully imbues.

Assessing Weblog use can be as easy as counting the number of blog posts a student publishes or as complicated as reading each post for form and content. I think it's unreasonable to grade every post that a student might make, but it may be reasonable to include every post in some overall assessment of effort. Also, students can self-select their best blogging posts, reflect on those selections, and include those reflections in an overall evaluation of their Weblog use. I've used a rubric to generally assess student work in the blog that evaluates the level of participation, the intellectual depth of the posts, the effectiveness of the writing, the level of reflection regarding the ideas expressed, and the willingness to contribute to and collaborate with the work of others.

What happens to the blog after the course ends is largely up to how they are being hosted and what district policy is. If students will continue to be able to have access to the sites, you may want to send a note home informing parents that this is the case. If you plan to take the sites down at the end of the year, give students a chance to save their work or perhaps transfer it to another service if possible.

BLOG SOFTWARE

From a software standpoint, a few basic considerations apply. If you are thinking about a software program that requires installation on a local server, you will want to make sure you have adequate tech support on hand to address any problems that may arise. Depending on what you choose, you or your support people may need to learn how to maintain the installation, back up the files on the server, and stay current on the latest updates. If you don't think you have enough tech support to run the program, you'll need to consider either going with a package that offers free hosting or purchasing hosting offsite from one of any number of Weblog suppliers. (More on specific programs later in this chapter.)

Regardless of what software you use, plan to take some time to dig into it and learn what its capabilities are. Even though most Weblog software makes is easy to get up and running, there are limitations as to the levels of security, collaboration, and ability to upload files. And if you're thinking about introducing Weblogs on a wide scale, plan to run small-group training sessions of 6–10 people at a time. Know, too, that documentation for most blogging packages is pretty slim. You might want to use your blog to keep track of the how-to information you dig up or come across in your travels.

The good news from a budget standpoint is that many blogging sites on the Internet offer their services for free, and there are a number of viable open-source packages that can be hosted locally. So, blogging doesn't have to break the bank. Again, the tradeoffs are level of security and ability to easily monitor what's being posted.

BLOGGING STEP-BY-STEP

So from the technical side, what's the best way to start blogging? Unfortunately, the perfect edu-blogging program has yet to be written, so this answer depends on what your needs and plans are.

Figure 3.1 Just click the arrow on the Blogger homepage to get started. (Used with permission of Google Inc.)

For a personal blog, and from an ease of use standpoint, I would recommend Blogger (www.blogger.com) which is owned by Google (see Figure 3.1). Blogger will host your Weblog for free, so you don't need to worry about setting up or maintaining software. It's also one of the easiest to use, and it has some levels of privacy that may make it worthy of consideration for a class blog as well. In fact, many teachers have used Blogger with their students with great success. Remember, you can create as many blogs at Blogger as you want from your one account, so you could manage a number of different sites from the one Blogger "dashboard."

Signing up for a blog at Blogger is as easy as advertised. The address of your site will be "http://whatevernameyouchoose. blogspot.com," so give some thought to what you want the first part of that address to be and be ready to try a few times to get a unique

Figure 3.2 Creating content on Blogger is as easy as clicking the "Create a New Post" button. (Used with permission of Google Inc.)

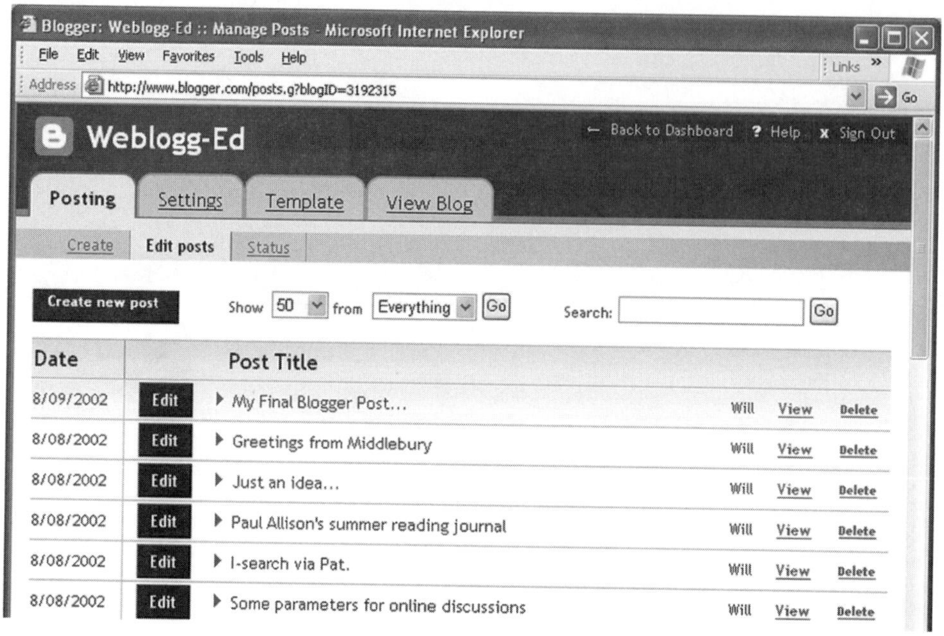

address that no one else has already chosen. Once you get through the sign up process the first time, remember you can always create another site by using the "Create a Blog" button on the Dashboard that comes up after you login.

When you click on a blog name from the Dashboard, you'll be taken to the page where you can create and edit posts depending on which tab is selected (as shown in Figure 3.2).

Just hit the "Create New Post" button to, well, create a new post to the homepage (Figure 3.3).

You'll be shown a form that has a line for a title and then a box for the post itself. Make sure you have the "Compose" tab on the top right of the box selected as this will give you the WYSIWYG (What You See Is What You Get) editor. Just give your post a title, enter in your content, format and create links by using the fairly standard icons along the top, decide if you want people to be able to comment, and then choose to either save it as a draft for editing later or publish it directly to your blog.

And there is a "Blogger for Word" tool now that allows you to post right to your blog from Microsoft Word (http://buzz.blogger.com/bloggerforword.html). The good news is that gives you the ability to spell check your post before publishing it, and it gives you an easy

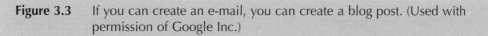

Figure 3.3   If you can create an e-mail, you can create a blog post. (Used with permission of Google Inc.)

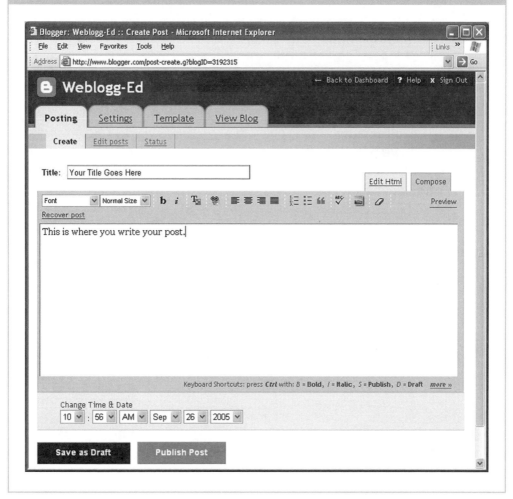

way of saving your work locally. Be aware, however, that not all of the formatting capabilities in Word will translate over to your Blogger site.

A note about comments: Under the "Settings" tab, there is a link to configure how you want your comments to work. There are three options: only registered users of Blogger (which Blogger hopes you'll check so they get more registered users), anyone who might read your post, or only people who are registered members of your blog. For that last one, remember that you have complete control over who those members are, as you are the one who invites them. (This is done by clicking the "Members" link under the "Settings" tab and then going through the "Add Team Members" process.) So if you are thinking about a blog that you can use to collaborate with colleagues or even students, that might be the best option you choose.

With student use, although Blogger does not directly give teachers the ability to approve student posts before publication, there is a way to work around this: Have students save all posts as "drafts" until they get the teacher's go ahead to publish. Or, the teacher could press the "publish" button himself. That way, nothing goes online without consent. Remember, however, for this to work, the teacher has to have full access to all student sites (not a bad idea no matter what blog software you use.) In Blogger, go to Members under the Settings tab and make sure the teacher/member is checked as an administrator as well.

You can always edit posts that you have created, even ones that you have published to the site, though most bloggers try not to do this. All of the posts on the site can be found under the "Edit Post" link under the "Posting" tab. You can even search your posts there, and you can choose to show as many posts as you want on that page.

One other configuration you'll want to make sure you choose is in the "Site Feed" link under the "Settings" tab. We'll talk much more about the importance of this in the chapter on RSS, but for right now, under the "Publish Site Feed" drop-down list, select the "RSS" option and the "Full" option in the "Descriptions" field (see Figure 3.4). This will allow people to "subscribe" to the content you write, making it easier for your ideas to spread, if you want them to.

The "Template" tab is where you would go should you want to roll up your sleeves and start editing the HTML code to change the look of

Figure 3.4 Make sure to enable your site's RSS feed. (Used with permission of Google Inc.)

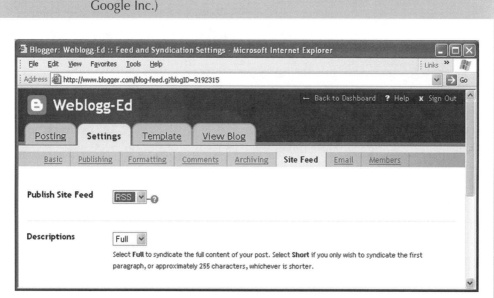

your page by adding links to the side column or adding a personal picture or changing the whole template. If you do this, be careful! The Blogger template has all sorts of code in it that makes your site work, and if you change any of it, you may render it inoperable. I would always suggest that if you're going to start playing with the template you first copy and paste the current, working code into a document that you can use to repair whatever you might mess up.

MAKING A BLOG ROLL

I'll just give you one little template tweak that will help you create a list of links that you might want to share with others. In most of the standard templates, you can scroll pretty far down in the template code and find a section that says <h2class="sidebar-title">Links </h2>. One of the links listed under that section should be <li><a href="http://news.google.com/">Google News</a></li>. If you use that line as guide, you can create as many links as you want by highlighting the entire line, copying it, pasting it, and then changing "Google News" to, say, "New York Times" and then replacing the Google News address with that of the *Times*. So it would look like this: <li><a href=http://www.nytimes.com/>New York Times</a>.

Adding pictures to your blog is easy now that Blogger gives you 300 MB of space on their servers. Just click on the image icon on the

Figure 3.5 Blogger also makes it easy to add pictures to your post. (Used with permission of Google Inc.)

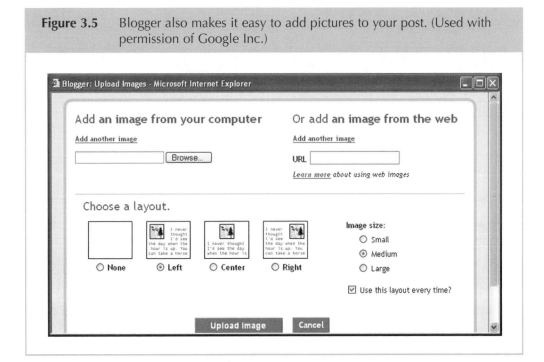

posting form and you'll be taken to a page where you can select pictures from your hard drive to include in the post (see Figure 3.5). Remember that your photos should be sized and formatted BEFORE you upload them. So if you need to rotate a picture or crop it, do so before letting Blogger take a copy of it. On the same page, you can also choose the URL of a picture that's already on the Web. (You can find the URL by right-clicking on any Web image and selecting "Properties.") Just copy the address and paste it into the Blogger form. Finally, choose a layout from the options, select the size you want the picture to be, and then click "Upload Image." It will automatically appear in your post. (By the way, you can add more than one image at a time by clicking the "Add another image" link on the image upload page; see Figure 3.6.)

Finally, you'll need to make one last adjustment to Blogger regarding safety. In the upper right-hand corner of the Blogger template, you'll see a link for "Next Blog." Unfortunately, that links to a random Weblog that might not be the most appropriate for a student to view. The good news is you can remove the button. Here's how: First, open up the main template. Next, find the <body> tag. Just in front of it, type <noembed> and right after it type </noembed>. That should solve the problem.

Figure 3.6 You can choose a picture from your computer or one already on the Internet. (Used with permission of Google Inc.)

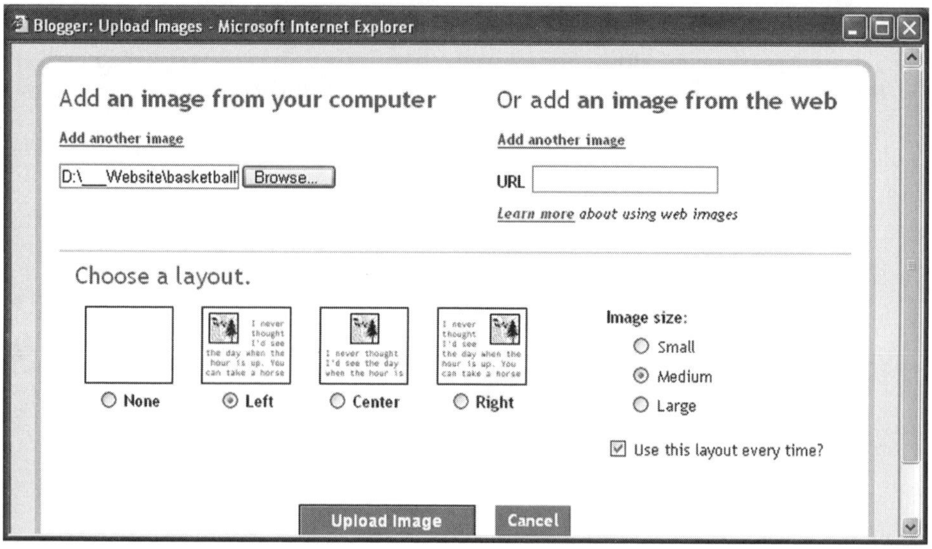

And that's really all you need to get started with Blogger. There are other free hosting services that you might consider, and a good starting point is the Weblogs Compendium (www.lights.com/weblogs/hosting .html). But if you want more functionality and greater levels of "control over what does and doesn't get posted, you'll probably have to consider using a different software program that you either pay to have hosted or host yourself. Again, the Weblogs Compendium is a good starting point.

Here is a list of some noteworthy options that you might want to consider:

Manila (http://manila.userland.com) is really a content management system with a Weblog tool built in. (Disclaimer: Manila is the software I use for my personal and school Weblogs.) It's a good choice if you are thinking about a large-scale implementation of Weblogs and can host them locally. Manila offers many levels of editorial control, allows teachers to approve posts, allows different audiences to see different posts, has a built-in discussion board and listserv, and even allows you to close sites to outside access. Cost is $499 a year for the license to run as many sites as your server will hold (in our case about 2,000). You will need to make sure you have the technical support necessary to maintain the server. If you want to give Manila a try before buying, you can create a free site at www.ManilaSites.com, which gives you a 30-day free trial.

WordPress is an open source solution that has gained a lot of traction of late. Like Manila, it gives teachers the ability to set permissions and access, and it allows them to approve work before it is published. Also like Manila, there are a lot of nice looking templates to choose from. Again, running WordPress on your local server may require some expert technical support. But you can find free WordPress hosting at a number of places, most notably from edblogger James Farmer at Edublogs.org and Learnerblogs.org.

Another favorite of teacher bloggers is *Movable Type*. Although some might find it a bit pricey at $700 for 1,000 students, it is a proven, well-developed, robust software that meets many of the privacy and safety concerns for educators. It's what Tim Lauer uses for his Lewis Elementary site that I mentioned before. You'll need your own server to host Movable Type, but if that's a problem, you might try TypePad (http://www.sixapart.com/typepad/), which is Movable Type in hosted form. For about $150 a year, you can create an unlimited number of multiple author Weblogs that are hosted by the company, and you can get all the benefits of Movable Type without the hassle. The only drawback, of course, is if the hosting service is down at the time you need it, you won't be able to just call your technician to get it up and running.

In addition, you might want to check out Kidzlog (http://kidzlog .com), 21Publish (www.21publish.com/), TeacherHosting (www. teacherhosting.com), Blogmeister (http://classblogmeister.com/) created by edblogger David Warlick (http://davidwarlick.com/2cents/), and the "Communities" software (www.nlcommunities.com) offered by educational consultant Alan November (www.novemberlearning.com) as alternatives. All have appealing characteristics for educators.

Here's a Blogger's Dozen of Good Educator's Blogs to Read:

Alan Levine (http://jade.mcli.dist.maricopa.edu/cdb)
Barbara Ganley (http://mt.middlebury.edu/middblogs/
  ganley/bgblogging/)
Anne Davis (http://anne.teachesme.com/)
David Warlick (http://davidwarlick.com/2cents/)
James Farmer (http://incsub.org/blog)
Stephen Downes (http://www.downes.ca/news/OLDaily.htm)
Tim Lauer (http://tim.lauer.name/)
Tim Wilson (http://technosavvy.org/)
Tom Hoffman (http://tuttlesvc.teacherhosting.com/blog/blosxom.cgi)
Ken Smith (www.mchron.net/site/edublog.php)
Jenny Levine (www.theshiftedlibrarian.com/)
Konrad Glogowski (http://www.teachandlearn.ca/blog)
Clarence Fisher (http://remoteaccess.typepad.com/remote_access/)

And with that, you should be well on your way. As you'll see, blogs are only one of many tools of the Read/Write Web, but I would argue they are the most important, and the most reasonable place to start your travels. No one knows what blogs may look like in 5 or 10 years, but I can tell you that no matter what, their impact and influence on education will be felt. Welcome to the blogosphere!

4 Wikis: Easy Collaboration for All

Imagine a world in which every single person on the planet is given free access to the sum of all human knowledge. That's what we're doing.

—Jimmy Wales, Wikipedia founder
(Wales, 2004)

If you want to find the most important site on the Web these days, look no further than Wikipedia.org (see Figure 4.1). As its name suggests, Wikipedia is an encyclopedia, one that really is attempting to store the "sum of human knowledge." In December of 2005, the English version of Wikipedia housed more than 865,000 separate entries with information about everything from the *Aabenraa* (a small municipality in Denmark) to *Zzzax* (a fictional supervillain from Marvel Comics). Every day, new entries are being added about people, places, things, historical events—even today's news almost as it happens. It's truly an amazing resource.

But whereas most people get the "pedia" part of the name, only a few really understand the first part, the "wiki." And believe it or not, that's the most important part, because without the wiki, this encyclopedia, this growing repository of all we know and do, could not exist. The word *wiki* is a short form of the Hawaiian *wiki-wiki*, which means "quick." The first wiki was created by Ward Cunningham in 1995, who was looking to create an easy authoring tool that might spur people to publish. And the key word here is "easy," because, plainly put, a wiki is a Website where anyone can edit anything anytime they want.

Figure 4.1   Wikipedia is the online encyclopedia that anyone can contribute to. (Retrieved from http://en.wikipedia.org/wiki/Weblog, retrieved September 7, 2005.)

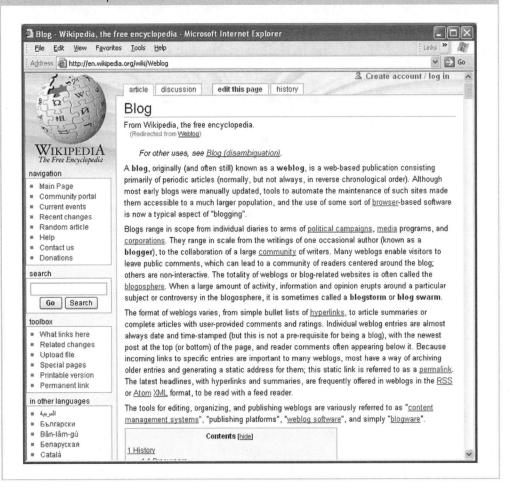

So, have some knowledge about your favorite hobby that isn't on Wikipedia? Add it. Read something you think isn't correct? Fix it. Don't like the way one of the entries is written? Erase it. Something big just happen in the news that is history making? Start a new entry. You have the power, because every time you access Wikipedia or most any other wiki for that matter, you do so as Editor in Chief. And it's that freedom that has made Wikipedia the phenomenon it is as tens of thousands of Editors in Chief, people just like you and me, take on the job of collecting the sum of human knowledge.

Most everyone's first reaction to that is that it sounds more like Whackypedia. "If anyone can edit anything on the site any time they want, how in the world can you trust what you read there?" they ask. It's a great question And some high-profile errors found in late in

2005 make it a relevant question as well.. The answer is that, thankfully, there are vastly more editors that want to make it right than those who want to make it wrong. So when mistakes occur or vandals strike, the collaborative efforts of the group set it straight, usually very quickly. University of Buffalo professor Alex Halavais tested this by creating 13 errors on various posts on Wikipedia, all of which were fixed within a couple of hours (Halavais, 2004). And in December 2005, the magazine *Nature* compared 43 entries in Wikipedia to the same entries in *Encyclopedia Britannica* and found Wikipedia to be only slightly less accurate (http://www.nature.com/nature/journal/v438/n7070/full/438900a.html). Pretty amazing, I'd say.

Now I know what you're thinking, something along the lines of "Well, I can skip this chapter, 'cause this anyone-can-do-anything wiki thing will never work in my school." But, try to resist the urge; wikis can be pretty amazing and versatile. And if you believe as I do that doing real collaboration is something that every student needs to learn, keep reading.

Take, for example, the Wikipedia entry created around the Indian Ocean earthquake that struck just after Christmas 2004 and created the tsunami that killed more than 175,000 people. The event occurred just after midnight (GMT) on December 26, and the first 76-word post was created at Wikipedia about 9 hours later. Twenty-four hours after the first mention, the entry had been edited more than 400 times and had grown to about 3,000 words, complete with some of the first photographs of the devastation, a chart documenting the dead and injured, and other graphics describing how the tsunami was spawned.

Forty-eight hours after the first post, the entry had grown to more than 6,500 words, had been edited 1,200 times, and included more than a dozen graphics including video of the wave itself. Six months after the event, more than 7,000 changes had been recorded, and the post had settled at around 7,200 words. All of it had been created and recreated by people just like you and me who were interested in contributing what they were finding to the entry. It was without question the most comprehensive resource on the Web about that horrific event.

That's how each of Wikipedia's more than 860,000 entries has evolved, from the hands of people just like us with the concept that everyone together is smarter than anyone alone. In the process, we check facts, provide "soft" security by acting like a community watchdog, and weed out bias and emotion from the posts in an attempt to arrive at a neutral point of view for each article. Each entry is the group's best effort, not any one person's.

In that way, Wikipedia is the poster child for the collaborative construction of knowledge and truth that the new, interactive Web facilitates. It is, to me at least, one of the main reasons I believe in the transformative potential of all of these technologies. No one person or even small group of people could produce Wikipedia, as currently edits appear at a rate of one every two or three seconds. Every day, thousands of people who have no connection to one another engage in the purposeful work of negotiating and creating truth. They do this with no expectation that their contributions will be in some way acknowledged or compensated, and they do it understanding that what they contribute can be freely edited or modified or reused by anyone else for any purpose. The extent to which this happens and to which it is successful is truly inspiring.

And the success of Wikipedia has spawned a wiki revolution. Not only can you contribute to the sum of human knowledge, you can add your favorite recipes to Wikirecipes (http://meta.wikimedia .org/wiki/WikiRecipes), your best vacation bargains to Wikitravel (http://www.wikitravel.org/), even your favorite spots for Buffalo Wings to, you guessed it, the Buffalo Wings wiki (http://buffalowings .wikispaces.org/). There's also Wiktionary, Wikinews, Wikispecies, and Wikiquotes. You get the idea.

Like blogs, wikis are beginning to make inroads in just about every area of life. Corporations like Disney, McDonalds, Sony, and BMW have started using wikis to manage documents and information. MIT, Stanford, and other colleges and universities are testing the waters with their faculty and students. The city of Calgary is using a wiki to let people share resources, experiences, and favorite diversions (http://calgary.wikicities.com/index.php/Main_Page). In fact, there are now tens of thousands of wikis growing out there for just about every reason imaginable including sites for everything from song lyrics (http://www.kiwilyrics.com/Main_Page) to Star Trek (http://memory-alpha.org/en/wiki/Main_Page). (In fact, the Start Trek wiki is one of the most impressive out there!)

In addition, wikis are also being used by project teams as a way to keep track of their work, by businesses who want their employees to share information and collaborate in an easy way, and teachers who want to collaboratively build resource sites for their classes. (Much more about that in a minute.) There are now even password-protected wikis that allow people to use the technology behind closed doors, and there are over 100 different wiki programs, most of them free via open source, that you can install on your server. In other words, just like blogs, wikis are coming of age.

So, how exactly do wikis work? Every page in a wiki has a link, usually at the top, that says "edit page" or something similar. When you click it, it takes you to the code behind the page. The vast majority of what you will see is simple, editable text. But there is some wiki code, which is a bit different from HTML. It might take a bit of getting used to the look, but using it is easy. (More about the specifics later on.)

Each page on a wiki also comes with another very important feature: a page history. The link to it is usually near the "edit page" link, and when you click it, you can see when changes were made, by whom, and what was changed. The best part is that if need be, you can easily use the history list to revert back to a previous version of the page should someone come and muck things up. This, in fact, is how most vandalism is dealt with, and what makes vandals give up. And from a technical aspect, that's pretty much all you need to know.

Philosophically, wikis can play havoc with the traditional ideas of copyright and intellectual property. Obviously, they follow closely the open-source software ideal that the quality of the collectively produced product is more important than owning the idea or the code. Really, wikis bring the concepts of open source to the mainstream as the ideas and process are no longer reserved just for software developers.

All of these challenges are great entry points for a discussion about the use of wikis in the classroom. As we continue to move toward a world where everyone has access to ideas and where collaboration is the expectation rather than the exception, wikis can go a long way to teaching our students some very useful skills for their future.

THE CHALLENGE OF WIKIPEDIA IN SCHOOLS

Before we talk about building our own wikis with students, a couple of more thoughts on Wikipedia. Already students are turning to Wikipedia as a resource for research, much to the chagrin of many teachers and librarians. As we've already discussed with blogs, knowing what sources to trust is becoming a much more labor-intensive exercise, and wikis, with many often anonymous authors, make that even more difficult. The idea that "it might be wrong" is a tough one for most people to overcome. Yet Steve Jobs, the CEO of Apple, has called Wikipedia one of the most accurate encyclopedias in the world (http://en.wikiquote.org/wiki/Steve_Jobs). What to do?

For one, teachers should spend some time checking Wikipedia's accuracy on their own. If your experience is anything like mine has been, you may end up agreeing with Jobs. But this still takes a faith that we didn't need in the days before the interactive Web, a faith that collectively we can produce information that is as high quality as what a trusted few produced in the past. It's a tough call. The early consensus among educators seems to be to tell students to use Wikipedia as a starting point for their work, but not as a sole resource.

The additional challenge with Wikipedia is that each of its entries is, in fact, a collaboratively written research report. It's not exposition in the sense that the entries are defending a thesis, just the opposite, in fact. But say you assign students to do reports on a specific country, Argentina, for instance. All the pertinent reporting about Argentina may have already been done and collected at Wikipedia. So in this case, is it more important for a student to be able to find that information and know how to evaluate it or to know how to repeat work that's already been done? Again, it's a tough call.

A final challenge is changing the way we think about the content our own students create. Should we be encouraging them to contribute what they learn and know to the Wikipedia entry on that topic? Think about it. If your student produces a great research paper on global warming, why shouldn't she add what she found to the global warming entry at Wikipedia? And why shouldn't we watch together to see what happens to that information that she adds? If it gets modified, we can think critically about those modifications. If it gets spammed (which is highly unlikely), we can come to the rescue. Either way, it can be a great learning experience.

If we begin to look at Wikipedia as another opportunity for our students to contribute what they learn and know to a larger audience, I think we can begin to appreciate it for the really incredible site that it is.

WIKIS IN SCHOOLS

So what about it? Are you ready to begin thinking about how a wiki might work in your classroom? Hopefully, despite the seemingly chaotic design of wikis, you're starting to imagine the possibilities here. So, before taking a look at the ways in which some forward thinking teachers have been using wikis in their classrooms, let's talk about some of the more obvious concerns. Namely, what would stop someone from anonymously going onto a class-run wiki and vandalizing it by erasing content or by adding profanities, for instance? There is no doubt that teachers on the K–12 level are going to be hard pressed to justify the use of such an open venue for the publication of student work, though, as we'll see, there are some that are doing just that. In theory, the "soft security" model could work in schools as well. If it's used as a group collaboration site a la Wikipedia, the class as a whole could monitor the content that is added and make the necessary edits and revisions. Giving students editorial control can imbue in them a sense of responsibility and ownership for the site and minimize the risk of someone adding something offensive. In fact, wiki projects in schools have worked best when the teacher loosens the reins a bit and lets students manage the content on the site.

As much as we'd like to trust our students to make good things happen, however, we all know that it would only take one parent to open the wiki and find something inappropriate to derail the project. The good news is that there are alternatives. Although wiki purists scoff at the idea, there are a number of Web-based wiki sites that feature a password and login system similar to Weblogs for people to interact with the site. Or similar software can be installed on your server and run locally. It's still a much more open and collaborative environment once inside, but in this way you can restrict who can and cannot access the site.

Wikis pose some pedagogical challenges as well. They can be so effective at fostering collaboration that the teacher really needs to carefully examine her role in their use. As I noted previously, early implementations of wikis in educational settings have shown that the more autonomy teachers give to students in terms of negotiating the scope and quality of the content they are creating, the better. It's a very democratic process of knowledge creation. In using wikis, students are not only learning how to publish content; they are also learning how to develop and use all sorts of collaborative skills, negotiating with others to agree on correctness, meaning, relevance, and more. In essence, students begin to teach each other. Teachers who impose a lot of right and wrong on that process can undermine the effectiveness of the tool. (For a further discussion of the pedagogical potentials see http://www.profetic.org:16080/dossiers/article.php3?id_article=970)

And remember, if the openness of wikis feels a bit too disruptive, wikis can be used in many other contexts inside schools as well. As we'll see, they can be used as collaborative tools among teachers or districts to collect and share information.

So how might we use wikis in our classrooms? One of the most obvious ways is to create an online text for your curriculum that you and your students can both contribute to. A co-construction of this type could make for a much more personalized text, one specific to your particular class. Or consider adding other students and other teachers who teach the same class. It could easily become a resource, a showcase for best practices, and an articulation tool as well. Students might use it to create their own class Wikipedia. If it's a physics class, for instance, students could post and edit entries that deal with the structure of the atom or ionization or . . . other things. (Remember, I was an English teacher.) They could add graphics and links, annotations and reflections. Just like blogs, they could also post PowerPoint presentations, video and audio files, and spreadsheets. And all of those collectively

Figure 4.2   The South African high school curriculum is being built on a wiki. (Retrieved from http:/en.wikibooks.org/wiki/South_Aftrican_Culture, retrieved September 7, 2005.)

assembled artifacts could serve as a starting point for future classes to then edit and add to.

Personally, the ability to easily amass and publish a wide-ranging, tailor-made resource like this is why I have a feeling that textbook manufacturers don't like the ideas of wikis one bit. Sure, they can always say that you can't trust a source that's not professionally edited. But in the era of the Read/Write Web, we are all editors, and we must all become skilled at doing that work. As these tools become more and more accessible, and as they continue to foster the publication and sharing of reliable information, it may not be long until traditional textbooks will fade into the background.

Don't believe it? Well try this on for size: the California Open Source Textbook Project (COSTP). According to its Website, "COSTP is projected to augment current K–12 textbook supply chain, be self-supporting with 18 months of starting up, and save the State of California upwards of $200M+ per year for K–12 textbook allocation within five years" (COSTP, 2005).

Or how about this: The entire national high school curriculum for the country of South Africa is now in a wiki (shown in Figure 4.2, http://en.wikibooks.org/wiki/South_African_Curriculum). The goal is to make it easy for teachers to share information on how to deliver certain lessons or achieve certain goals with their students. What a concept, huh? Can you imagine what that resource could become?

This is happening on an even wider scale at Wikibooks, where almost 10,000 textbook modules have been created in just 2 years (http://en.wikibooks.org/wiki/Main_Page). Which brings up another way that you can use wikis in your classroom: have your students create or edit entries to books that have already been started elsewhere. Introduce them to the concept of a wiki, show them how it works, have them pick an entry to edit, review their edits with them, have them share the link when their work is posted, and then have them track their edits to see how others might edit them. It's a great opportunity to introduce students to the concepts of open source software, community collaboration, respect for other people's ideas, intellectual property and public domain, and much more.

EXAMPLES OF WIKIS IN K–12 EDUCATION

Among the teachers using wikis in schools, few have done more than Paul Allison at East Side Community School in Manhattan. Paul, who is also a blogger (http://nycwp.org/paulallison/), has created an incredible wiki site (shown in Figure 4.3, http://schools.wikicities.com/wiki/Main_Page) that involves the work of about 100 students and teachers who are creating entries about everything from bulimia (http://schools.wikicities.com/wiki/Can%27t_Keep_It_Down%3F) to basketball (http://schools.wikicities.com/wiki/Basketball). In addition, the wiki serves as the online place for staff and community news, art shows, sports teams, and much more.

On his own blog, Paul says, "To write in a wiki is to compose within a living organism" (Allison, 2005). As students approach the wiki with writing ideas in mind, they first search to see if content about that topic has already been posted. So they need to read critically first, if they are to find the areas where information is missing or disorganized. Even though the writing is not their own, they must take it as their own because they have the ability to edit and make it better. This is a huge shift.

Figure 4.3   Paul Allison uses a wiki with his high school students to teach collaborative writing skills. (Used with permission of Paul Allison.)

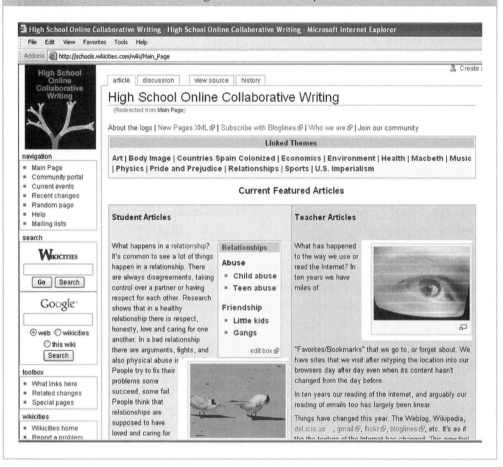

As students interact with the wiki, they are learning not only about collaboration but about publishing and writing as well. Here is an example. Carlos, who is a sophomore, thinks the Yankees' Alex Rodriguez is the best baseball player in the majors. So, he created a page in the wiki (http://schools.wikicities.com/wiki/Alex_ Rodriguez) where, with a template created by Paul, he's writing an argumentative essay to that effect. Other students can then also edit the post. (And if you want a great deconstruction of how all this works, check out Paul's blog posting on December 4, 2005, at http://www.nycwp .org/paulallison/2005/12/04)

"It's interesting when students are really reading something and thinking about how to change it," Paul says. "And it's different in that instead of saying 'I'm against abortion,' they have to figure out how to say that 'some people are against abortion.' The community builds the argument, not any one person" (P. Allison, personal communication, April 26, 2005).

He has also been excited by how many of his students have gone in and added posts on their own, posts about the environment and other topics that concern their lives. He says that despite the openness of the site (no login required) there has been very little vandalism, although he does monitor the posts very closely via the history list.

Another example is the Holocaust Wiki Project (http://www .ahistoryteacher.com/holocaust/tiki-index.php) developed by Dan McDowell for his students at West Hills High School in Santee, California. First, groups of students develop the outlines of a family living through the Holocaust based on historical and geographical research. Then each group sets up a number of choices that the family must make, annotates each choice with pros and cons, and asks the reader to make one of the choices to see what happens. For instance, a Jewish family may at first have the choice of trying to run or following the Nazi instructions to report to a camp. Depending on the choice you make, you're faced with another decision, and as the reader makes these choices, the narrative of the family is written. Each of these choices are added to the wiki as a separate page and then woven together via links into a self-selected story.

The process for developing this simulation demands some fairly complex thinking and planning; if you're at all interested in this project, take some time to read through it. The wiki facilitates the whole process. "Using a Wiki allows [students to] easily create web pages . . . edit each others' work, and easily link the pages together," Dan writes (McDowell, 2005; http://www.ahistoryteacher.com/holocaust/tiki-index.php?page=About+this+Project). I think it's a great use of a wiki, where page creation is easy and creating a webbed narrative like this can be a really fascinating experience.

Another great wiki idea was spawned by Rob Lucas, a sixth-grade teacher from North Carolina who created the Teacher's Lounge (http://teacherslounge.editme.com/). Basically it's a site where any teacher can come and leave a lesson plan for other teachers to share. Rob is trying to "develop an extensive library of creative, finely tuned, engaging, exciting lessons." A similar, more local wiki for teachers in your district might be an equally interesting idea.

And then there is Planet Math (http://planetmath.org/), which is "a virtual community which aims to help make mathematical knowledge more accessible." This is a dynamic community of math educators that is collaboratively creating a mathematics encyclopedia (a la Wikipedia), and anyone can participate. (Just sign up to become a member.) Currently there are more than 4,400 entries, ranging from abelian to Zsigmondy's theorem, neither of which I remember studying in school. In this case, each entry has an "owner" that reviews any changes on a regular basis, but the concept is the same.

So let's take a minute and imagine the possibilities here. Your students, with just a little help from you, could create book report wikis, what-I-did-this-summer wikis, brainstorming wikis, poetry wikis, notes-from-class wikis, sixth-grade wikis, history-of-the-school or community wikis, formula wikis, wikis for individual countries they might be studying, political party wikis, exercise wikis . . . you get the idea. And you could create similar spaces for colleagues to save research or do articulation or much, much more. Whatever topic might lend itself to the collaborative collection of content relating to its study, a wiki is a great choice.

WIKI TOOLS FOR SCHOOLS

If you want to give wikis a try in your classroom, you may want to start at the Peanut Butter Wiki site shown in Figure 4.4 (http://www.pbwiki.com). The bad news is you and your students will have to share a password, so you won't be able to track who is doing what unless they include their first name or identifier when they login to the wiki. The good news is, if you like, only you and your students will be able to access the site, and, of course, PB Wikis are free. You can create as many as you want, so think about small-group wikis as well. To create your site, just type in the name you want for your wiki on the top line and an e-mail where a confirmation and password can be sent. When you get the e-mail, just click the link back to your PB Wiki site, enter the password that was sent to you, and you're off. That's it!

The first thing you'll want to do is change your password to something you'll remember. Use the "Admin" tab at the top of the page and then click on the Change Password link. And remember, if you want your students to collaborate on the site, you'll need to give them the password as well. With PB Wiki, only the site creator can change the password, so if for some reason outsiders get access, you can slam the door on them.

Under the "Admin" tab you'll also be able to set whether or not you want the wiki site to be public (a nice option to have), and you can save a copy of your wiki as a backup, something you should probably do on a regular basis, just to be safe.

When you're ready to start building your wiki, you might first review the "WikiStyle" guide that is linked from your homepage. (Note: Almost all of the different wiki software have what's called a

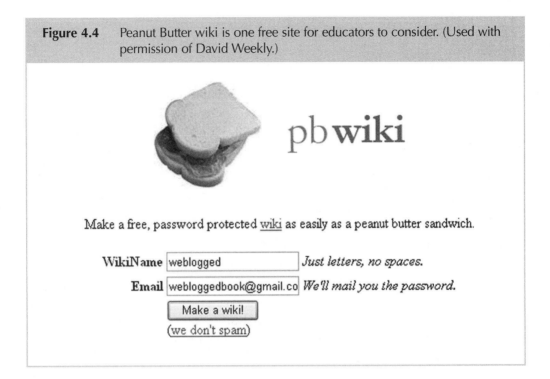

Figure 4.4   Peanut Butter wiki is one free site for educators to consider. (Used with permission of David Weekly.)

Make a free, password protected <u>wiki</u> as easily as a peanut butter sandwich.

WikiName | weblogged | *Just letters, no spaces.*
Email | webloggedbook@gmail.co | *We'll mail you the password.*

Make a wiki!
(we don't spam)

"Sandbox" to play around in before you actually start creating.) To make a new page in PB Wiki, you simply click "Edit" on the home-page and, in the text box that appears, add a word that has two capital letters with small letters in between: for example, FirstPage. That's the form that all new page links take. When you "Update" your edits, you'll see the word "FirstPage" is now a link on your homepage. Simply click the link, and it will take you to a text entry box where you can start entering your content. Remember, those MashedTogetherWords are what you use to build your site. Every time you need a new page for something, just CreateAName. And then anywhere you put that MashedTogetherWord in your wiki, it will link to the relevant page. Try it . . . it's easier than it sounds.

Just as a note, with other wiki software, it may be the bracket ([ ) that is the mechanism for creating links and new pages. An example of this would be the Wikicities site that Paul Allison uses. Let's say, for instance that you were starting a wiki about everyone's favorite baseball team, the Chicago Cubs. If you want to create an entry for every player on the team, you click "edit page" and then start typing their names in brackets, like this:

[Mark Prior]
[Kerry Wood]
[Nomar Garciaparra]

When you save the page, the text will appear like this:

Mark Prior?
Kerry Wood?
Nomar Garciaparra?

The question marks are links, which when you click on them will take you to new pages created for that particular player. When you add content to those pages, the entire names on your homepage will automatically turn into links and the question marks will disappear. That's how you build your wiki site: create the link, then create the page. Like most free blog software, you'll need to get your files and pictures up onto the Internet before linking to them in your wiki.

Once you have your pages rolling, remember that you can add files or, alternatively, links to files that are a part of the class. Ourmedia.org (for files) and Flickr.com (for pictures) are made for this. To make pictures appear, just add brackets around the URL of the image. Making links to files or other unique URLs is a bit different, but still not as hard as HTML. Separate the URL and the name you want to give the link with a vertical line, and then put brackets around the whole thing. So if I wanted to make a link to Wikipedia, for instance, I would enter: [http://en.wikipedia.org/ | Wikipedia].

If you want more control over what gets entered and by whom, you might want to try JotSpot (http://www.jot.com). It's much more feature rich than PB Wiki, and it will let you assign individual logins and passwords to the people you choose to participate. Right now, this service is free for up to five users and 20 pages. So you may need to create a series of wikis that you could conceivably tie together using a blog. From a teacher-only standpoint, JotSpot is a great tool.

Signing up for a JotSpot account is similar to PB Wiki. Click on the "Create Pages" icon on the homepage and follow the procedures. Once again, you'll need to confirm your account via e-mail. Once set up, take some time to go through some of the tutorials and documentation in the "Help Quick Links" in the right column. One nice difference between JotSpot and PB Wiki is that Jotspot uses a WYSIWYG editor that makes adding and changing content a breeze. (WYSIWYG stands for "what you see is what you get," so this editing system makes edited content appear in the same format as the final version on the page.) And creating new pages works the same way; MashWordsTogether and then click on the links they create to start putting content on the page.

But the great feature of JotSpot is the membership function. From the "More Actions" drop-down list at the top of the page, select

"Add/Manage Users." This will take you to a page where you can enter the student's name, her e-mail, assign her a password, and more. This way, every time she comes to add or change content on the site, she'll be logged in under her name and you'll be able to see the edits she's made. To track what edits have been made to the site, just click on the "Revisions" link at the top of the right-hand column. If you want to revert back to a previous version of the page, just click on the link to view it, click edit, and then click save.

JotSpot is much, much more than a wiki, however, and it would take a separate book just to go through all of the applications it features. It has everything from a blog to a checkbook register, so if you like what you see with the wiki, you may want to dig into it a bit more deeply.

OTHER WIKI TOOLS AND RESOURCES

As I said before, there is a whole slew of different wiki programs that you can choose from if PB Wiki or JotSpot doesn't fit the bill. The best list that I've found is the Wiki Engines list at http://c2.com/cgi/wiki?WikiEngines (Note: You may want to visit the site with whoever runs your servers).

Some other free tools to check out are SeedWiki.com and Wikicities.com. Both offer free wiki hosting with varying levels of permissions and access.

Finally, there are a few other interesting and cool wiki-type tools I'll mention that you might want to take a look at. First, there is WebNote, which is like an online Post-It Note repository (http://www.aypwip .org/webnote/). Basically, you go to the site, create a page name in the form, and click "load" to get started. You can add a Post-It by clicking the little yellow icon in the upper left and then double-clicking in the yellow post-it-type box that appears. You can include basic HTML inside the boxes, and you can color code your notes for easy sorting. All of your notes are totally searchable, so you might want to think about creating some standard tagwords to add as you go along.

But the coolest thing about WebNote is that you can easily save snippets of text from Webpages you might be visiting. Here's how: The first time you go to your notes page, type "B" and a note will appear with a link for a bookmarklet. Drag the link to your "Links" toolbar on your browser, and the next time you're visiting a page and you find some text you want to save to your WebNote page, just highlight it and click that link. Automatically you'll be taken to your note page and you'll see your highlighted text in a box with a link to the source. Cool, huh? If you want to edit that note, just double click it.

Now why is this a wiki? Because anyone who knows where your page is can come in and add, edit, or delete notes. That's right, anyone. Good news is that makes it easy to share the space. Bad news is, well, you know the risks by now. But again, if someone comes in and destroys the content on the page, you can always revert back to the last correct version. So, although WebNote may be a bit too open for student use, you could create a WebNote page for group study or research with other teachers, and you can even subscribe to the RSS feed for that page to monitor what they are posting.

Or try Web Collaborator, which is a free wiki and blog tool that allows you to invite members to participate with three levels of access (http://www.webcollaborator.com). The "Project" is the wiki, and it has all the basic tools you'd want in terms of a history of updates, a WYSIWYG editor, and easy revisions. The "Discussion" is the blog that you and your collaborators can use to plan or update each other on the status of the wiki. It's a simple, fast little tool that has some powerful uses for student groups, and it too has an RSS feed.

Last but not least, if you're using Firefox as your browser, there is the Wikialong plug-in. Believe it or not, by using Wikialong you can leave a note on any page on the Internet so that when anyone else comes along while using Wikialong, they'll be able to add to it. What a concept.

Regardless of how educators feel about the potential of wikis, and I can understand the hesitancy many teachers feel, one thing remains certain. The collaborative environment that wikis facilitate can teach students much about how to work with others, how to create community, and how to operate in a world where the creation of knowledge and information is more and more becoming a group effort. I'm serious when I say that I get chills sometimes when I think about the amazing work that's being done at Wikipedia. In many ways, it gives me great hope for the future because it is a testament, I think, of good people doing good. Using wikis, we can start to show our students what it means to be a part of that process.

And if the wiki bug does bite you as it has me, this might come in handy:

> Please, grant me the serenity to accept the pages I cannot edit,
>
> The courage to edit the pages I can,
>
> And the wisdom to know the difference
>
> —The Wiki Prayer
> http://www.educause.edu/pub/er/erm04/erm0452.asp

Have fun!

5 RSS: The New Killer App for Educators

True or false: Weblogs, wikis, and their friends (which we'll get to later) are creating so much more content on the Web that there's just no way to keep track of it and find the relevant stuff you need to know?

If you said true, you're half right. (Which, of course, means you're half right if you said false, too.) The ability of average Joes and Janes to easily create and publish content to the Internet certainly is creating an avalanche of information that feels absolutely overwhelming. But the good news is that the tools of the Read/Write Web are not just focused on publishing. There are also a few tools aimed at helping you consume all that information in more efficient and relevant ways. Meet RSS.

RSS stands for Real Simple Syndication and if you're an educator, I think it's the one technology that you should start using today, right now, this minute. And tomorrow, you should teach your students to use it.

In simple terms, Weblogs (and an ever-growing number of other sites) generate a behind-the-scenes code in a language similar to HTML called XML. This code, usually referred to as a "feed" (as in "news feed"), makes it possible for readers to "subscribe" to the content that is created on a particular Weblog so they no longer have to visit the blog itself to get it. As is true with traditional syndication, the content comes to you instead of you going to get it, hence "Real Simple Syndication."

For instance, say you're a political science teacher and you've found 20 or 30 Weblog and media sites on the Internet that are consistently publishing interesting and relevant information for you and your students. Finding the time to click through to those sites and keep abreast of any new information on a regular basis would be nearly impossible. But what if you only had to go to one place to read all of the new content on all of those sites? Wouldn't be so difficult, would it? Well, that's exactly what RSS feeds allows you to do by using a type of software called an "aggregator" or feed collector. The aggregator checks the feeds you subscribe to, usually every hour, and it collects all the new content from those sites you are subscribed to. Then, when you're ready, you open up your aggregator to read the individual stories, file them for later use, click through to the site itself, or delete them if they're not relevant. In other words, you check one site instead of 30 . . . not a bad tradeoff for a typically harried teacher.

Here's another scenario: You currently get the headlines from the *New York Times* via an e-mail message that arrives each morning. But more and more, your e-mail box is being clogged up by spammers selling everything from pornography to mortgages. There are new virus warnings every day. That *New York Times* content is getting lost in the morass that e-mail has become. Not so with RSS. The *New York Times,* as well as hundreds of other newspapers, magazines, television stations, and the like, has a number of virus-free "feeds" that your aggregator can collect. And in general, you know that everything in your aggregator is something you want to read because you subscribed to it. No ads, no spam, just new content from the sources you read.

So, Reason #1 to get your brain wrapped around RSS? You can read more content from more sources in less time. In fact, you may even be able to cancel the subscriptions you have to paper versions of magazines and newspapers that come to your nondigital mailbox. With RSS, you can create your own collections of news and features that are personalized to your interests.

But there is an even better reason, I think, to use RSS. Not only can you have the news and ideas of the day come to your aggregator. You can also use RSS to let you know when someone out there on the Web has published something with certain keywords that you might be interested in. So, by using RSS, you can create a feed for "global warming New Jersey" that will bring new results as they are published right to your online mailbox.

Now think for a second about what that means. Students can be immediately updated when new information about research topics is published. Teachers could track the blogosphere for discussions about motivating students or the unique pedagogies of the class. Superintendents could be notified about what's being written about their schools. Once again, the possibilities are . . . well, pretty interesting.

RSS is a technology that will change your life, if you let it. Over the last couple of years, I've been able to track about 150 feeds of information daily, from bloggers, newspapers, search engines, and more. Over that time, I have read or skimmed literally tens of thousands of posts and developed a fairly keen eye for quickly spotting the most relevant and interesting information. And that is another one of those skills that our students, the knowledge workers of the future, are going to have to develop in order to flourish. Given the fact that the amount of information going online shows no sign of slowing, if they are unable to consistently collect potentially relevant information for their lives and careers and quickly discern what of that information is most useful, they will be at a disadvantage. And, as with the rest of these changes, it's our job to model and teach these skills.

So we're going to cover a lot of ground in the next few pages, but before we do, a bit of advice: Go slowly. If you really want to understand the potential of RSS, take a week or two to work through the techniques in this chapter. None of them are particularly difficult, I promise. But the results can be a bit overwhelming. Don't be surprised if at first you think RSS is adding to your information overload instead of easing it. With a little time and experience, you'll begin to understand why pretty soon RSS will be a household tool, and why it will make you and your students smarter, more effective consumers of information.

SETTING UP AN RSS FEED READER

Ready to start? First, you need to set up an aggregator to collect your RSS feeds. I would suggest the Web-based service from Bloglines.com. Why?

Although there are a number of great downloadable newsreader packages out there that can do wonderful things, the main advantage to Bloglines is that you can access it from anywhere you have an Internet connection. In other words, you don't have to be on your own computer with special software installed to read your news. (Of course, if you do only use one machine, there are many aggregators with more features than Bloglines that you may want to consider. Check out http://en.wikipedia.org/wiki/News_aggregator.)

Setting up a Bloglines account is easy. When you get to the site, use the "Click Here to Sign Up!" link in the middle of the page and follow the procedures. You'll get a confirmation e-mail to which you'll need to respond, and then you should be ready to go.

Bloglines has a few ways to subscribe to feeds. First, you can look at their listing of most popular subscriptions by clicking on the "Find New Blogs" link under the "Cool Features" section of the Bloglines homepage (or just go to www.bloglines.com/topblogs). It will take you to a page of the 150 most subscribed-to feeds among their users. You can preview the content, and then, while you are logged in, you can subscribe to any on the list by clicking on the "Subscribe" link under each feed description. Then, click on the "My Feeds" link at the top left of the screen, you'll see the feeds you subscribed to with the number of messages waiting to be read in parenthesis next to the name. Any time you come back, the feed name will be bold when new messages are waiting (see Figure 5.1).

The other way to subscribe to feeds is to manually add them to your list by using the "Add" link at the top of your subscription list. Remember this: A feed address is really a URL or web address. You find RSS feed addresses in the same place you find the address to any Website you might visit. So, to subscribe to a feed in Bloglines, you'll need to paste the address of the feed you want into the subscribe form that appears on the next page. For instance, if you wanted to track the new content on my blog, here is the RSS feed to my site: http://www.weblogg-ed.com/xml/rss.xml (much more about finding feeds in a second).

Once you paste in the feed address, Bloglines will ask you if you want to make a folder and whether or not you want other people to see that you've subscribed to that content. (You have the option of letting others view your subscriptions. My public feeds are at http://bloglines.com/public/wrichard.) And, when you have some feeds to work with, Bloglines lets you rename them (among other things) by clicking on the "Edit" link at the top right of the right-hand frame when you are viewing the results of one of your subscriptions. It's pretty intuitive, and if you start getting quite a few feeds in your list, you might want to take the time to get organized (the "Reorder/Sort" link is useful for that as well).

Now before you do anything else, put a link to Bloglines on your toolbar or in your Favorites folder. If you want up-to-the-minute results, add the Bloglines notifier (www.bloglines.com/about/notifier) to the bottom of your screen, which will let you know when new

Figure 5.1 In Bloglines, make sure you paste the address of the RSS feed into the "Subscribe" form. (Used with permission of Ask Jeeves, Inc.)

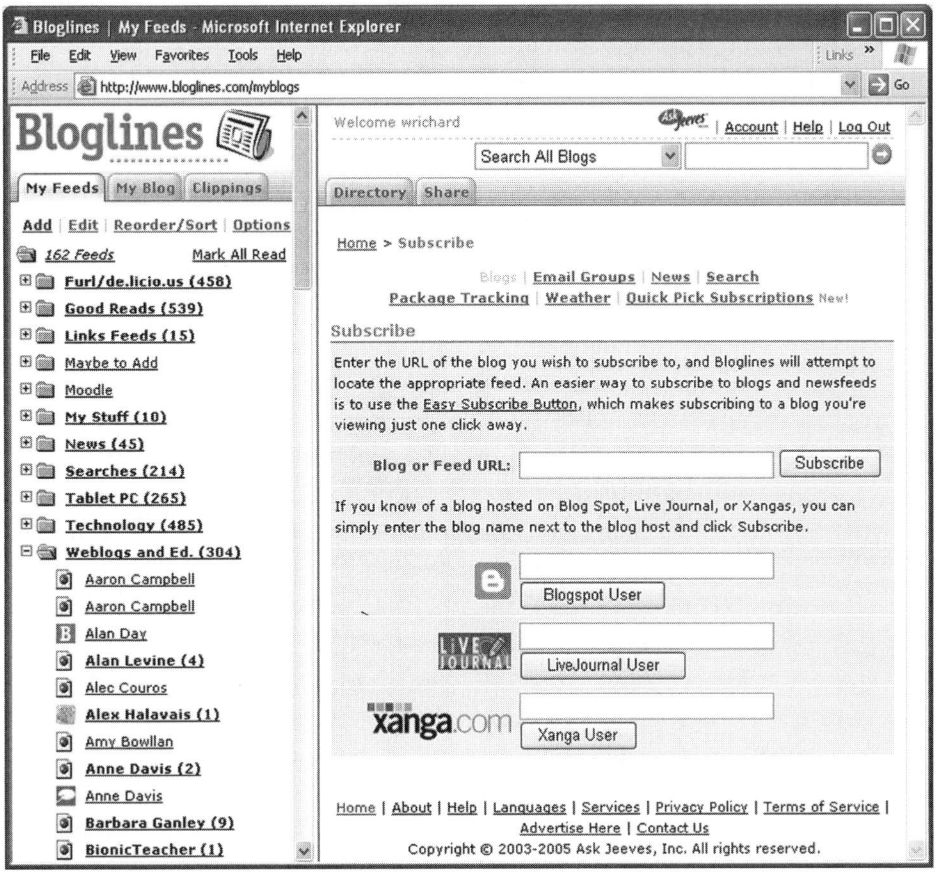

content has been posted to any of the feeds you are subscribed to. Either way, remember to check back often. Collecting feeds only works if you read the new stuff regularly! (For even more info, read the Bloglines FAQ at www.bloglines.com/help/faq#updates.)

FINDING AND ADDING FEEDS

Once you have your aggregator set up, it's time to find some relevant feeds to stock it with.

For the moment, let's just deal with blogs. First, understand that most Weblogs have a link to their feeds on their homepages. On many, it's a text link in one of the side columns that says "Syndicate this site (XML)." Or it might be a link that says "RSS 1.0 (or 2.0)." But most often, it's a pretty orange icon that looks like this: XML "This is a link to this site's RSS channel: Weblogg-ed News." No matter which type it is, you'll need to click on it in order to get the address of that site's feed. Don't worry if the page that comes up is a scary looking mass of code that you can't make heads or tails of. Remember that all you really need is the Internet address of that page (the URL.) Just copy the address, go into Bloglines, click the "Add" link and paste it into the subscribe line at top of the right hand window, and subscribe. Next time you visit your "My Blogs" page, the feed for that site should show up.

If you're not sure what Weblogs to subscribe to, you can always use one of the blog search engines to find sites that might be relevant to your interests. Some of the better Weblog search sites include Technorati.com, Feedster.com, and Daypop.com, but there are many more listed at Weblogs Compendium at this page: www.lights.com/weblogs/searching.html. Just put in some search terms that represent your interests, click through the results to a few blogs, and spend some time reading. And once you've found a few blogs and added them to your aggregator, Bloglines will also recommend some other feeds that you might be interested in based on what you're already reading. (Isn't that nice of them?) Just click on "Recommendations" at the bottom of your subscription list.

Luckily, you can subscribe to much more than blogs, however. More and more news outlets and standard Websites are adding feeds for their content so, there will be more and more to choose from in the future. The list at RSS Compendium includes feeds from newspapers, magazines, governments from around the world, schools and universities, businesses, and many more sources (http://allrss.com/rssfeeds.html).

Finally, you may just want to put in the name of your favorite publication and/or commercial entity into a search engine with the word "RSS" to see what comes up. For instance, a quick search of the soon-to-be World Champion Chicago Cubs and RSS brought me to four sites that have feeds I can subscribe to. Heaven.

USING RSS FEEDS IN THE CLASSROOM

So, you've got your favorite Weblog and media feeds in your aggregator, and you're starting to get the hang of this "getting the good stuff when I want it" concept. How can you start using this in your school and in your classroom? Well, there are a number of different ways that RSS feeds can add to your knowledge base, help you communicate, and make your teaching better.

RSS Feeds With Student Weblogs

If you already use Weblogs with your students, the uses of RSS should be pretty apparent. Instead of checking out all 25 (or 30, or more) student Weblogs every day, you could just collect their work in your aggregator using their RSS feeds. That way, you can scan through all of the class content in one place, make sure it's all appropriate, and click through to a particular post if you want to comment on it. My use of student feeds in this way has drastically reduced my reading time and allowed me to make all of my classes paperless. In addition, you can provide individual student Weblog feeds to parents or counselors or whoever else might be interested in that student's work and be savvy enough to know about RSS. (Don't worry, pretty soon most people will know.)

With some Weblog packages, you can even subscribe to feeds that show new comments on the various sites, or even to just certain topics. In other words, you can track just about everything going on in your student blogs using RSS.

In addition, Weblog software like Movable Type and Manila allow you to import RSS feeds into pages you create for your or your students' sites. Although it takes a little bit of code to make it work, the benefits of bringing topic-specific feeds right into student (or teacher) work spaces are something that you might want to explore. (See also the "Including RSS Feeds in Your Weblog" later in this chapter.)

RSS Feeds Without Student Weblogs

Even if your students don't have Weblogs, you may want to have them set up their own Bloglines account. With more and more news sources producing feeds for aggregation, the breadth of current events and even topic-specific research that students could collect could go a long way to assisting them with research or further study. (It's one reason why I think RSS could be a great help for the lack of media and information literacy skills students have.) And, if you use a Weblog, they can include your feed in their aggregator to stay abreast of what is going on in class.

RSS Search Feeds

The idea of creating RSS feeds for search terms is especially interesting. Say you have a student that is doing a project or a paper on mad cow disease. That student could actually create an RSS feed that would bring any news about the disease to his aggregator as soon as it was published. Kind of like doing research 24/7, only the RSS feed does all the work. And you can create a feed about any topic you want. Here's how:

RSS Feeds for News Searches

Both Google News and Yahoo News have recently made it possible to track standing searches with RSS feeds. And they've both made it very easy to boot.

Let's start with Google. Just go to news.google.com and click the "Advanced Search" link above and to the right of the search form. Here you can add the words you want to search for, the location you want them from, and even a particular publication. (Google has about 4,500 news sources that you can choose from, and although Google does not publish this list, you can find a growing list of Google's sources at: www.privateradio.org/blog/i/google-news/index.php?ord=count.) Click the "Google Search" button and see what you get. If the results aren't really what you were looking for, you may need to come back and modify your search.

If, however, the page of results looks pretty relevant, all you need to do is click on the "RSS" link in the left column of the page. Take the really long URL of the messy page of code that comes up and paste it into your Bloglines account. From that point on, any time there is something in the news about the topic you searched for, the result will show up in your aggregator. And remember, you can create as many of these feeds as you like. If you ever want to stop receiving the feed, just delete it from your aggregator. (If only we could do that with spam, right?)

Ok, say you're not a Google lover and would rather use Yahoo News instead. It's just as easy. Just go to http://news.yahoo.com, put in your search terms, and look for the little orange XML icon in the right hand column. (You may have to scroll down.) In fact, Yahoo has some amazing tweaks to this process that will let you limit the region the news comes from, the language, and even category. Basically any parameter you want to enter in an advanced search can be saved to an RSS feed. To me, that's pretty amazing. See the Yahoo Search Blog for more details (www.ysearchblog.com/archives/000039.html).

RSS Feeds for Weblog Searches

Getting a regular feed of searches in the blogosphere is just as easy, but you need to remember that the results aren't always going to be as, shall we say, appropriate. Obviously, the vast majority of Weblogs are not edited for content by someone other than the author, and invariably there will be some questionable posts that will land in your aggregator. Still, Weblogs offer up some really great potential research, and you might want to experiment with searching them on your own before bringing students into the fray. To do so, the easiest way is to go to Feedster.com and type in your search terms. On the page of results, you'll see a little 2.0 RSS box that when you click on it will give you a number of standard newsreaders to choose from. If you're logged in at Bloglines, just click the Bloglines link and it will automatically add it to your account. Otherwise, click on the 2.0 RSS box and grab the URL from the next page. You can go through pretty much the same process at Bloglines, Blogdigger.com, Syndic8.com, pubsub.com, and other Weblog search sites.

Another option is Technorati.com which is a leader in indexing weblog content. Once you've signed up for a free membership, you can create what Technorati calls "Watchlists." Each watchlist you create has it's own RSS feed that you can add to Bloglines. And, Technorati is also in the business of following the way people "tag" or characterize their posts. So let's say you wanted to track all of the posts that bloggers have labeled "classroom." Just go to http://www.technorati.com/tag/classroom and look for the RSS feed link at the bottom of the page. Obviously, you can substitute any keyword you like at the end of the address above.

RSS Feeds for Website Searches

There's more. You can even create an RSS feed from a search of Google sites (not Google news, sites.) So, if there is new content about global warming added to a site that's already on the Internet, or if there is a whole new site created about the topic, you'll find out about it in your aggregator. Here's how. Go to Googlealerts.com and sign up for an account. It's free. Once your registered, you can create up to three searches that can bring back up to 150 results total. Just fill in the form with the search terms you want, click "Go," and then click "Feed Settings" on the next page. All of your searches will come up, and you can check the box that says "RSS Feed" next to each one of them, then click "Update" at the bottom. Then, take the feed address that appears in each box and copy it into your Bloglines account. (No page that comes up with that scary looking mass of code that you can't make heads or tails of this time.)

MSN search now sports RSS feeds for the results as well. Just go to http://search.msn.com/ and type in your search. At the bottom of the results page you should see one of those orange XML buttons. You know what to do by now . . .

RSS Feeds for News Group Searches

You can also search Internet news groups and get an RSS feed of the results. (Where does it end?) To do this, go to Pubsub.com—the specific address is http://www.pubsub.com/newsgroups.php—put in your search terms, and click "Create My Subscription." On the next page, either click on the little Bloglines icon to add it to your aggregator, or copy and paste the subscription link that is provided. Pretty cool. But beware that a search feed of newsgroups can bring back all sorts of irrelevant content, so you may want to spend some time refining your search to match your interests.

RSS Feeds for Other News Outlets

Another way to get continually updated news about various topics is to use the feeds provided by Moreover.com. It provides a huge list of predefined topic searches at http://w.moreover.com/categories/category_list_rss.html. You can find even more of these types of Moreover feeds (including ones for your favorite sports teams, the state you live in, and your favorite presidential candidate) at this page on the Syndic8.com site: http://www.syndic8.com/feedcat.php?Scheme=Syndic8

RSS Feeds for Bookmarks

Feeds are also a great way to keep track of what other people are reading and bookmarking for future use. But to understand that concept, you'll have to wait until the next chapter on "The Social Web." You'll be amazed at the information you can collect.

Vanity Feeds

A good way to start building your blogging community is to find other bloggers out there who have similar interests and are writing about similar themes. One sure way to spot a blogger like that is to find one that's blogging about you! It's easy to track what other people might be saying about your blog by being alerted whenever someone is linking back to you. The easiest way to do this is to create a watchlist at Technorati for your blog address. But you can also do this at Feedster.com, BlogPulse.com, PubSub.com, and others. That way you can use your Bloglines account to find out when you're a part of the "distributed" conversation that is a hallmark of the Read/Write Web.

COMBINING RSS FEEDS

Now let's say you have a classroom full of students who each have their own Weblogs. They also have set up accounts at Furl so that they can collect relevant Web pages for the work they are doing, and they have a number of search feeds that they are tracking to collect even more information. From a teaching standpoint, if you wanted to monitor all of that information flow, it would take quite a bit of time and work. But here is a way to combine all of those collective feeds into one so that you can keep all the related work together and get a clearer picture of a student's work flow.

Blogdigger.com (http://www.blogdigger.com) has a way to create what they call groups of feeds, blending as many different feeds as you want into one. Just go to the Blogdigger site, click on the "Groups" button, click on "Create a New Group," fill out the information on the form that follows, then on the next page enter the various feed addresses that you want to combine. Blogdigger gives this new feed a unique address that you can then take and use in Bloglines or however else. Or you can try RSSmix.com where you just plug in as many different feeds as you like into the form, press "Create," and put the resulting feed into your aggregator, or as we'll see in the next section, somewhere else where it might be useful.

INCLUDING RSS FEEDS IN YOUR WEBLOG

Even though using Bloglines or some other aggregator is the easiest way to collect and view your feeds, with a little bit of work you can actually get feed results to show up on your Weblog or other Web page. Some Weblog packages have built-in ways to do this, and the instructions vary. But I'm going to show you one way to create a piece of Java script that you can then take and drop into your page wherever you want to put it.

This little "Feed to JavaScript" tool comes courtesy of Alan Levine, who is the tech guru at the Maricopa Center for Learning and Instruction in Arizona and who writes the Cogdogblog Weblog (http://jade.mcli.dist.maricopa.edu/cdb). You can find it at http://jade.mcli.dist.maricopa.edu/feed/index.php?s=build. Just enter the feed you want to display, fill out a few more parameters, and voila, the JavaScript is created for you. Just take it and drop it into the HTML of your blog, and your feed results will start showing up right on the page.

READING RSS FEEDS

Ok, so now you have hundreds . . . er . . . dozens . . . um . . . a few RSS feeds in your aggregator or maybe even distributed on different pages on your Website. Now comes the hard part: checking the feeds. The real job now is to make Bloglines (or whatever other aggregator you choose to use) a part of your daily practice. Maybe you check it right after you check your e-mail. Maybe you make it your computer's homepage for a couple of weeks. Or maybe you tape up reminders in your workspaces. However you do it, you need to build up a habit of checking to see what's new on a daily basis.

If you do stick with it, you'll begin to notice some changes in the way you go about getting your information. First, odds are you'll find yourself buying fewer newspapers and magazines. I can't tell you how much money I've saved since I started building my own "Daily Me" in my Bloglines account. Second, you'll find that as you get more and more used to the process, you become very good at scanning the text and finding the relevant or interesting stuff without reading every word. RSS could stand for "Reading Skill: Scanning" or "Reading Skill: Synthesizing" or . . . you get the idea. And this is a very important skill for our students to learn as well. As I've said, they are only going to be more and more inundated with information, and if they can learn early on to create more relevant connections to the ideas and sources they need and then be efficient readers, it will serve them very well in their futures.

RSS is a powerful, flexible tool that I think will be changing our information gathering habits for years to come. If you don't try any other tool in this book, you simply have to start using RSS. Remember: Resistance is futile.

Here are some cool RSS feeds to get you started:

Airport Delays via RSS: http://www.pubsub.com/airports.php

Weather via RSS: http://www.rssweather.com/

Earthquake Notification via RSS: http://www.pubsub.com/earthquakes.php

Techbargains via RSS: http://www.techbargains.com/rss.xml

Word of the day via RSS: http://dictionary.reference.com/wordoftheday/wotd.rss

Ebay via RSS: http://www.rssauction.com/

6 The Social Web: Learning Together

It was always there
But it could be found nowhere
Now it has been furled.

—Zen & the Art of Furling
(Cuyahoga County Library, 2005)

Whether it's blogs or wikis or RSS, all roads now point to a Web where little is done in isolation and all things are collaborative and social in nature. As evidenced by wikis, the biggest most sweeping change in our relationship with the Internet may not be as much the ability to publish as it is the ability to share and connect and create with many, many others of like minds and interests. These social connections, these "Small Pieces Loosely Joined" as author David Weinberger so eloquently put it in the title of his book, are where the real power and potential of the Read/Write Web lies for educators and students. The collaborative construction of knowledge by those willing to contribute is redefining the ways we think about teaching and learning at every level.

The social Web says that we have many friends out there just waiting to be found and connected to, and those friends have other friends (friends of a friend or "FOAF") who can just as easily connect with us and point us to new and interesting information or learning. You can almost visualize this network of individual nodes of people, connected by ideas and passions, constantly shifting and changing as new connections are found and old ones are reconsidered. Finally, it also means that we're willing to share our ideas and resources with the network for its betterment, because we get back just as much if not more.

This vision is much different from the traditional classroom in which most student work is done in isolation, never finding connection to a larger whole that might be produced by the class in its entirety. That's not to say that in this new world students don't do their own work. But it does mean that responsibility for that work is in some way shared by those interacting with it, the readers and commentators from within the classroom or outside, if allowed. Learning is a continuous conversation among many participants.

With blogs and wikis, obviously, these social interactions focus on the creation of content and meaning. They can be collaborative spaces where people negotiate and construct meaning and texts. But there are other tools that are being borne out of the Read/Write Web that focus primarily on creating connections rather than creating content.

Here's an example. At 43Things.com, your students can go and create a list of 43 things they want to learn or accomplish or do. Once they have created their list, they are automatically connected to everyone else within the 43 Things universe who want to learn those same skills or accomplish those same goals. So, let's say you want to learn how to play guitar. Instantly, 43 Things connects you to the 192 (at this writing) other people who want to learn guitar as well. (There are about 3,200 people who want to stop procrastinating . . . what are they waiting for?) And they even create a unique discussion place just for you and your group complete with an RSS feed. (43 Places.com works the same way, hooking you up with people who want to go or have been to places you want to go.)

Worldwide almost 1 billion people are now online, and the ways in which they are connecting and creating together are literally exploding. The power of social interaction, as evidenced by Wikipedia for instance, is immense, and is being harnessed in all sorts of new and creative ways. And, once again, the implications for teaching and learning are significant as well. Because of these tools, we can build complex networks of resources to tap into, allowing us to find more information, more teachers, and more learning.

SOCIAL BOOKMARKING SERVICES

With more than 10 billion pages of information on the Web already and millions more being added each year, it's no wonder people are starting to feel overwhelmed by the Internet. Search engines like Google and Alta Vista do a good job of helping find what we might be looking for. But as we all know, sometimes their algorithms to determine what's most relevant or important don't always hit the mark. And even though we now know that RSS feeds can help us track new hits to those search terms, they suffer from the same limitations. It's starting to feel like you need your own army to help you keep track of all the information you might need or want.

Well guess what? The army has arrived. Millions of people have begun using public, online bookmarking services where they can save links, annotate them with unique keywords or "tags" to organize them, and then share them with the world (Figure 6.1 shows some typical tags). So, for instance, if you find a great site that lists the 50 best free software programs for teachers, in the process of saving the link to your personal account, you might attach the words "education," "software," "free stuff," or whatever else you find relevant. What these services do that's social is take all of the entries that are tagged the same way and connect them, and then connect all of the people who posted those links in the first place. So if I bookmarked a site and tagged it "free" and "software," odds are pretty good we would find each other and learn from each other's efforts. Suddenly, it's easy to find all sorts of other people who have the same interests or passions as you do. And in doing so, you're creating your own community of researchers that is gathering relevant information for you. So, social bookmarking sites complete the circle: RSS lets us read and connect with what others write; now we can read and connect with what others read as well.

Take this example from a social bookmarking site named del.icio.us that we'll talk more about later. Let's say you run across Edugadget.com, which is a great site for teachers looking to incorporate the newest technologies into their classrooms. You want to find out what other sites might offer similar information. When you bookmark this site at del.icio.us, you'll immediately be linked to everyone else who has also bookmarked Edugadget. Now most people added the tags "education" and "technology" when they saved the link. But here are some of the other tags that people have used when saving Edugadget: "blog," "edu-blog," "web," "tech," "edu," "tool," "learning," "elearning," "blogging," "reviews," "media," "info," "teachers," "educational," and

Figure 6.1 Tags or keywords are becoming the tools that we use to organize our own pieces of the Web.

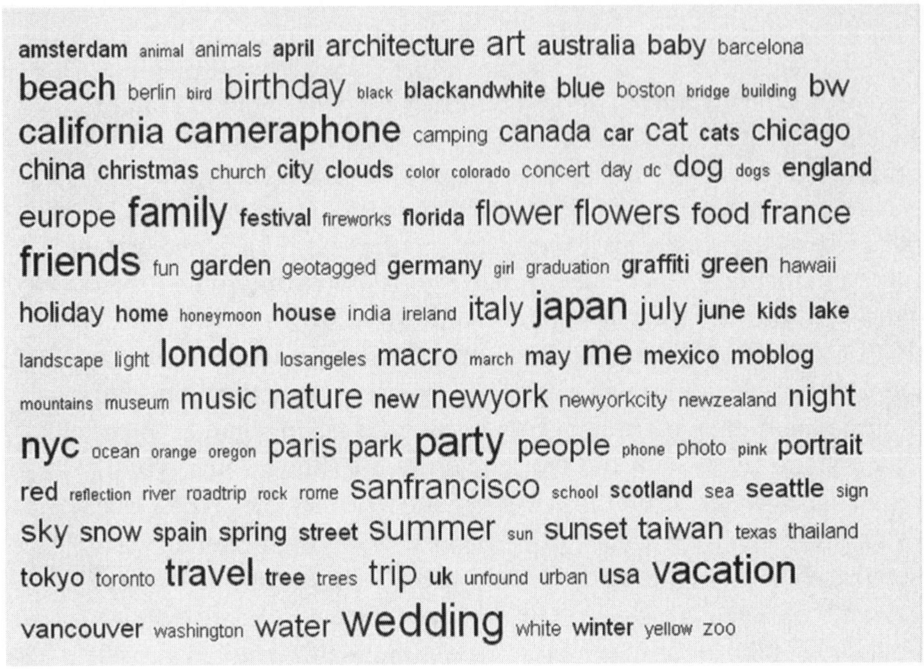

amsterdam animal animals april architecture art australia baby barcelona beach berlin bird birthday black blackandwhite blue boston bridge building bw california cameraphone camping canada car cat cats chicago china christmas church city clouds color colorado concert day dc dog dogs england europe family festival fireworks florida flower flowers food france friends fun garden geotagged germany girl graduation graffiti green hawaii holiday home honeymoon house india ireland italy japan july june kids lake landscape light london losangeles macro march may me mexico moblog mountains museum music nature new newyork newyorkcity newzealand night nyc ocean orange oregon paris park party people phone photo pink portrait red reflection river roadtrip rock rome sanfrancisco school scotland sea seattle sign sky snow spain spring street summer sun sunset taiwan texas thailand tokyo toronto travel tree trees trip uk unfound urban usa vacation vancouver washington water wedding white winter yellow zoo

"technologies." del.icio.us gives you the ability to click on any of those tags to be connected to other resources that might be similar to Edugadget. The community points the way.

But there's more. In the process of creating this community, you are participating in the creation of a new way of organizing information as well. This is another one of those dramatic shifts the Read/Write Web is bringing about. Back in the old days, we used to rely on librarians and others to sort and categorize information for us. These traditional taxonomies have been with us for a long time and they worked well because the sorting was being done by trained professionals who used a consistent process. That's why we're usually able to find what we're looking for in a library or on a subject-specific search site like Yahoo! But today, when we now have the power to organize vast libraries of information on our own, the process is being run by millions of amateurs with no real training in classification.

Not to worry, however, because as with many topics on the new Net, users of social bookmarking systems have created a new concept to deal with the change: The process is no longer taxonomy but "folksonomy." The idea is that in working with your community of researchers, new tagging systems will emerge and become accepted that will allow us all to participate in the process. Although this might be seen as chaotic and not as effective as traditional methods, by being able to apply many tags to one particular link we get the added potential of seeing how others might interpret or use resources that we share. Thus we get connected to information in ways that traditional libraries cannot duplicate. And the more people contribute in the creation of folksonomies, the more valuable they become to all who participate.

And it won't end there. The idea of tagging our own content is spreading, to digital photography (as we'll see later with Flickr), to multimedia, even to documents and presentations. The more such "metadata" that we can apply to the content we create, the more easily it will be connected to other relevant artifacts, continuing the process of joining the many pieces of the Web in flexible and dynamic ways and bringing us closer to the information we need and desire.

This move toward a more socially negotiated categorization of content has interesting and, I think, powerful ramifications for teachers and students. Obviously, if we are to be expected to participate in the construction of "folksonomies" to save the information that we find, it will require us to redefine the processes we currently use in relative isolation. Our personal organizational systems for content may need revision to fit with a more communal model. And it's worth our while to do this because this more social model has the potential to lead us to more and better information. But social bookmarking also challenges us to rethink the way we and our students treat the information we find. Traditionally, we emphasize keeping track of where our research comes from. But in this new construct, it will become even more important to know how to retrieve it within the folksonomies created with our community of researchers (Educause Learning Initiative, 2005).

Now there are many of these social bookmarking sites that have been created in the past couple of years. But two, Furl.net and del.icio.us, have come to the forefront of the pack for some very different reasons. Once again, these are both free services that any teacher or student can access on the Web. As with other sites, although the content you'll find here is primarily safe and in good taste, take the time to become familiar with both before you use them in the classroom.

Let's start with Furl, which is yet another one of my favorite tools on the Read/Write Web. To me, Furl, which is owned by LookSmart, is a tool that you can use to construct your own personal piece of the Web. I use it to store sites that deal not just with education and technology, but for sites related to journalism, parenting, environment, kids, and the "state of the world." Whenever I find something that interests me, I "Furl" it and add it to my archive of sites. I have thousands of sites saved, and I find myself coming back regularly to retrieve ideas or quotes. (In fact, Furl has been invaluable in the writing of this book.)

As with most of these tools, setting up a Furl account is easy. Just go to the site and click on the "Create Your Free Account" link. Pick a unique username, and because you might want to share this with your students at some point, pick something they might remember. You'll get an e-mail validation to confirm your registration. Once you've set up your account, you need to add the "Furl It" link on your toolbar. Just drag the link from the Furl homepage up to the toolbar area of your browser and it will create a button that you'll click on every time you find a page to save. (You'll need to do this for every computer that you go online with.) If for some reason your school blocks your ability to add links to the toolbar, just right click it and select "Add to Favorites" (Internet Explorer) or "Bookmark this Link" (Firefox). Then, when you want to Furl something, you just click on the link from your traditional favorites or bookmark list.

Here are some of the really neat features that I think set Furl apart. First, when you save a site in your Furl account, you don't just save a link, *you save a snapshot of the entire page.* That means that if one of your favorite sites were to suddenly disappear from the Web, you would still have a copy of whatever pages you Furled in the past. It means the end of "linkrot," which is what happens when pages get taken down, moved, or changed and your links to it no longer work. To me, that's reason enough to be Furling. Obviously, some question the legality of saving pages from a copyright standpoint. But even though the links you save become accessible to others, only you can access the saved page from your archive. Basically, you are saving a copy just for yourself.

But, of course, there is much more. The fact that Furl is Web based means that you can save from any computer and retrieve from any computer that has Internet access. Just like Bloglines, I find this to be extremely convenient. (As you can tell, I'm a big fan of Web-based applications.) At any time, you can do a full-text search of any of the pages you have saved, and you can also search the tags or, in Furl's case, "keywords" that you assign to whatever you are linking.

Furl actually gives you a couple of ways of categorizing your links. Aside from keywords, you build topic folders in which you can file related sites. For instance, using the Edugadget example from above, I could put it in my "Tools" folder and my "Edblogs" folder (shown in Figure 6.2), but I could also add whatever keywords I want to more accurately describe it. I might add "training," "software," and "cool," for instance. And, when I save the link, I can also enter a description or capture a piece of the text on the page. See the Furl save dialog box for all of the other information you could add.

Figure 6.2   Furl lets you capture a variety of information about a page, including a picture of the page itself. (Used with permission of LookSmart, Ltd.)

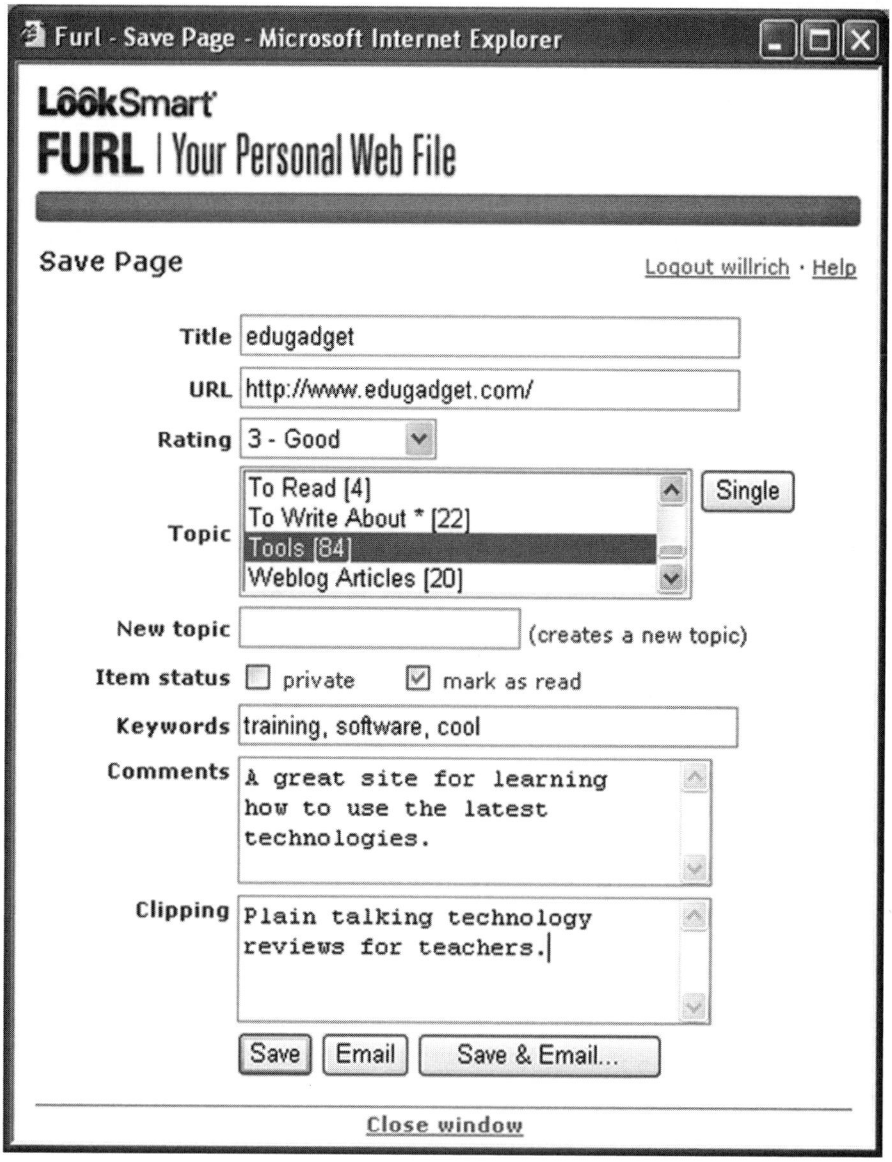

You can also search the entire Furl community for keyword matches, which is the first of many social features of the site. Obviously, once you find a result that looks interesting, you can click through to see the saved page, see the live Website, or see a list of other people who have also saved it. Click on any of their names, and you'll be taken to a page that lists the latest links that have been saved by that person. There you can also find the list of folders they are using to file their links. The idea, obviously, is to find other "Furlers" who are finding and linking to sites that you find relevant and interesting. It's like someone else doing research for you.

Now this is where the fun starts. Furl gives you all sorts of ways to track what other people are reading and saving. Here's one way it might work. Say you're teaching *Romeo and Juliet*, and you come across a great resource site for the book. When you "Furl It," you see that a dozen other people have also saved the site. When you click on one of the user names, you find that person has a whole folder dedicated to *Romeo and Juliet* resources. Great! But guess what? Now that you know all about RSS, it should come as no surprise that you can subscribe to that person's *Romeo and Juliet* folder. Just open it up, click on the little RSS icon at the top of the search box, take the address of the page that comes up and go add it to your Bloglines account. Then, any time that person Furls a site about *Romeo and Juliet*, you'll be notified. This is where the true power of social software combined with RSS lies.

Ok, now let's think about this some more. What if you set up a Furl account for your class of students? (I'm going to assume all of your students have Bloglines accounts by this point.) First, you could have your students subscribe to the feed of a particular folder you created just for that subject. That way, any time you link and comment on a site that you've found relevant to their study, they'll automatically get it too (see Figure 6.3). Even better, you could create separate folders in your Furl account with each student's name and have that student subscribe to the RSS feed for it. That way, every time you run across something you think Meredith might be interested in reading, you simply Furl it into the "Meredith" folder and her feed will automatically update. Think about how you could put the comments feature to good use in this example. You could insert individualized questions or other links or suggestions for follow-up. In this way, you can start to use Furl as a powerful tool for individualized instruction.

Or, if you feel comfortable, create an account in which all share the login and password and let them start saving links relevant to whatever you are studying into a class archive. As a part of the process, start building your own socially negotiated folksonomies in terms of keywords. In fact, you could ask them to add their first names as keywords and in that way be able to track who is adding what. Or, if you want to make sure you know who is doing what, have all of your students start their own Furl accounts. Create a unique keyword that they can add to each site that they save, like "RJ101" for that *Romeo and Juliet* example. Then you can go into Furl, search the community archive for "RJ101," and subscribe to the RSS

Figure 6.3 If you create a separate Furl folder for each of your students, they can automatically be notified when you save a bookmark for them. (Used with permission of LookSmart, Ltd.)

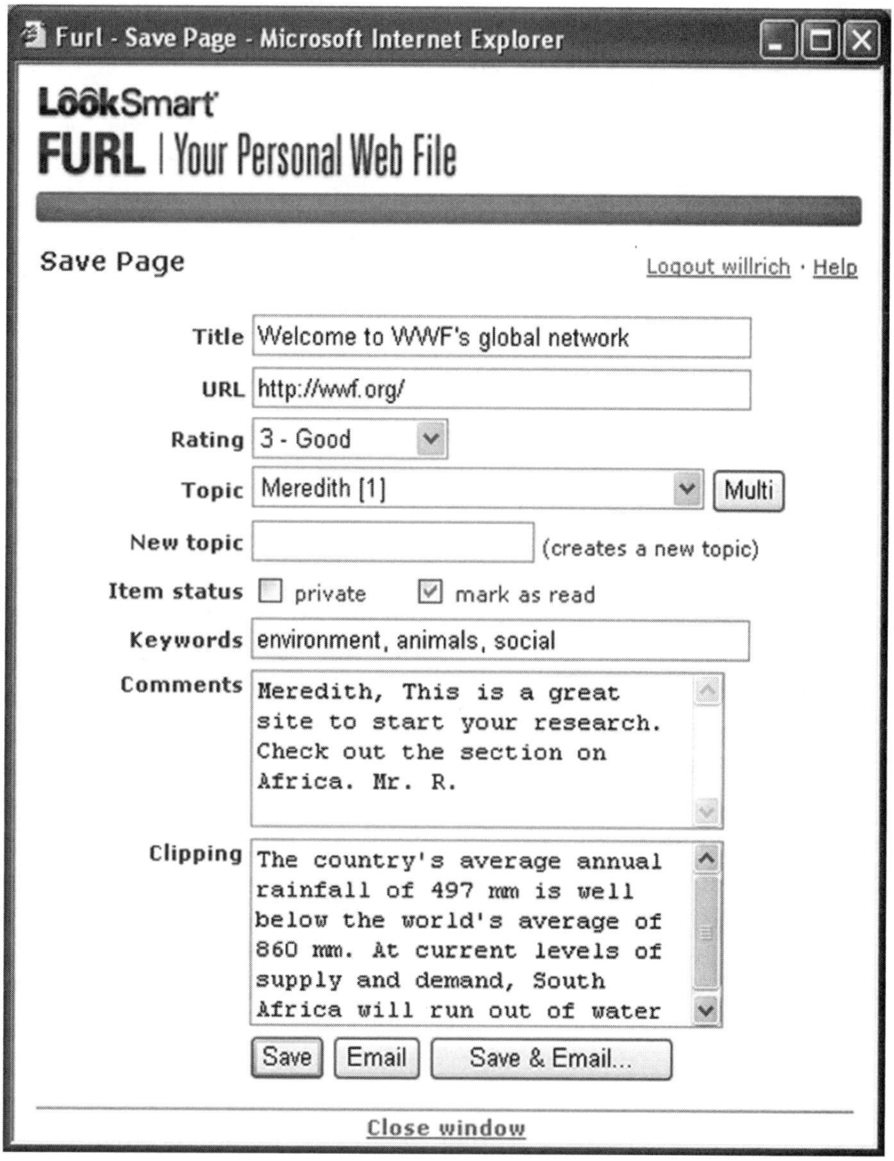

feed for the results. That way anytime one of your students Furls a site, you'll not only be notified, you'll know who saved it.

Individual student Furl accounts are a no-brainer for students' own research projects as well. Not only can they save and archive their sources, they can pull out relevant quotes right into the form, and they can organize the information by topic or subtopic. And the best part from a student standpoint? When they are all finished, Furl has a way to export all of the sources they used in MLA format (or APA or Chicago or CBE). Just click on the "My Tools" tab and select the "Export" link. (While they're there, they might want to back up their archives by exporting it to their local drive as a .zip file as well, something all Furl users should do on a regular basis.)

That's how Jim Wenzloff, a technology consultant for the Macomb Independent School District in Michigan uses Furl when training teachers and running classes. Using the export feature, he easily creates handouts (online or paper) of the resources he has Furled for the class. And in his work with preservice teachers, he simply subscribes to their Furl feeds, which come complete with their comments, to see what they are reading (Wenzloff, 2005; you can check out Jim's guide to using Furl at http://www.classroomhelp.com/workshop/furl_guide.pdf).

Furl is also a great way of sharing information with colleagues. If you are in a school in which four, five, or even eight people are teaching Political Science, either set up a Furl account that you can share in terms of adding resources or, at the very least, create folders in your individual accounts that you can each subscribe to. It's a great way to develop a highly personalized, organized, searchable archive of information for your curriculum. (And because Furl also gives people the option of subscribing to folders via e-mail notification, even those who might be a bit RSS wary can join in the fun.) Better yet, if all of your students have their own Weblogs, how hard would it be to set up a "Best Practices" folder in which you Furl exemplary work to share with parents, administrators, or counselors.

And let's not understate the importance of Furl as a professional development tool. Just getting in the habit of saving interesting or useful links can be a huge asset in and of itself. And Furl allows you to mark individual links or whole folders as private, so you can use the same account for personal reasons as well.

You can also add Furl feeds to a particular Webpage. At our school we use it to automatically excerpt relevant and interesting stories about education right to our parents' page. (Refer to the RSS chapter for details on how to do this.) It's just one more way of finding and sharing information with a minimum of effort.

del.icio.us, on the other hand, approaches the social bookmarking concept a bit differently. Whereas Furl is about saving content, del.icio.us is all about sharing links in as easy a way as possible. But although it may not have all of the flexibility and power that Furl has in terms of search and archiving, its simplicity makes it an equally powerful tool for teachers and students.

To del.icio.us, the tag is everything. Literally. One look at the save dialogue box tells you that aside from the site address, the most important piece of information is the label or tag you give it. Yes, you can add some annotation to the link, but finding and connecting to relevant information is not done through search; it's done through the tag. So any description you add to your link will be just for your own use. If you want to find what anyone else has saved using the same tag, just put the tag word at the end of the following address: http://del.icio.us/tag/yourtaghere.

Like Furl, the folks at del.icio.us are kind enough to provide RSS feeds for all of their tags. And the feed address is almost too simple. If I want to follow what people are saving about education, for example, the URL for my Bloglines account is http://del.icio.us/rss/tag/education. Just replace the last word with whatever term you want to follow and you have your feed address. So really, you could do this without ever visiting the site. (By the way, most often, tags that are more than one word usually use an underline to separate the words. So, classroom Weblogs would be tagged as classroom_weblogs.)

Like Furl, you can make this work to your advantage by creating unique tags that you share with your class or colleagues. And you could create a unique tag for each student in your class that they in turn could subscribe to so the links you save for them would end up in their personal aggregators. Remember, however, that there is no way to prevent others outside the class from using the same tags when saving their own links. (If you make it unique enough, however, the chances will be minimized.)

del.icio.us is so Google-esque in its minimalist design that it doesn't even require an e-mail address to register. Just put in a username, add (or make up) your real name, create a password, and you are good to go. This makes it extremely easy to use with students, if of course, you trust them to behave appropriately. On the other hand, it also makes it easy for you to set up student accounts, subscribe to the individual feeds, and then give them the information they need to login. This way they are responsible for whatever content appears in their links list.

Just like with Furl, teachers who use del.icio.us successfully think a lot about the tagging folksonomy they set up. You could have students all tag their links with RJ101 as in the example above; any tag will work for collaborative class efforts as long as it's unique. Here's an example from a community college chemistry class: http://del.icio.us/chem130.

Now, not to overwhelm you, but sites like Furl and del.icio.us have spawned all sorts of add-on tools to make your process even more interesting, flexible, and hopefully enjoyable (http://pchere .blogspot.com/2005/02/absolutely-delicious-complete-tool.html).

Furl and del.icio.us work well as social bookmarking tools because they both have a very substantial user base. But there are other tools that, as of this writing, are looking to compete in unique ways. One of those that I like is Jots.com, which basically takes the best of Furl and del.icio.us and combines them. Jots will save a copy of the page like Furl, and it lets you assign tags to each post like del.icio.us. Like Furl, you can annotate your links with as much copy as you want, and like del.icio.us, it's very easy to create and subscribe to RSS feeds. Add to that a very clean, blog-like style with a list of your personal tags within easy reach, and I think Jots has some real potential.

To sign up for a Jots account, all you need is an e-mail, a user name, and a password. Like the other two, you can drag the Jots bookmarklet to your browser toolbar to make it easy to start saving links. You can also add a button that will tell you if anyone else has "Jotted" a page you are viewing at the time. And whether you want to track everything that's posted to Jots, just the links of one particular user or tag, or just links that contain a certain search term, there are little XML buttons everywhere that make subscribing to the RSS feeds very, very simple.

But one really interesting thing you can do with Jots is set up private groups. What this means is that you and your students could collaborate to save links in a space that only you would see. You can invite other Jots users to share this function as well, so conceivably you could have your own private community of links in the making.

If you want your students to learn the benefits of social bookmark-ing but don't like the thought of using public tools like Furl or del.icio.us, there are some alternatives. ScuttlEDU, for instance, is an open-source links manager that will run off your own server and allow you to restrict access (http://blogs.zanestate.edu/mybook marks/help.php). de.lirio.us is another (http://de.lirio.us/rubric). Both of these tools make the concept available to younger kids in a safe way.

And, if you find yourself wanting to use more than one of these tools simultaneously, check out the Multipost Bookmarklet Tool created by Alan Levine (http://jade.mcli.dist.maricopa.edu/alan/ marklet_maker.php). With just one click, you can save a particular link to Furl and del.icio.us and over a dozen other social bookmark-ing sites that you may choose to use.

But regardless of how you do it, the idea that we can now use social networks to tap into the work of others to support our own learning is an important concept to understand. It's another example of how the collective contributions created by the Read/Write Web are changing the way we work and learn.

7 Fun With Flickr: Creating, Publishing, and Using Images Online

The easiest place for teachers and students to begin experimenting with creating and publishing content other than text is with digital photography, a technology that is becoming more and more accessible every day. Fairly high resolution digital cameras can be had for as little as $100 these days, and most are easy enough for even elementary school students to use productively. Even camera phones can shoot pictures that are of a high enough quality to be used in the classroom. And simple software to edit and resize these photos is available for free on the Web. In short, teachers and students can now include digital images in their list of things they can create in the classroom.

More importantly in the context of the Read/Write Web, there are a growing number of ways to publish these photos to the Web easily and cheaply. In fact, some of the best photo hosting sites offer free hosting for quite a large number of photos, and they allow users to create albums and multimedia shows that can be shared with friends and family.

But it doesn't end there, and from an educational standpoint, this is where the real fun starts. Imagine not only being able to put your or your students' photos on the Web to share with other audiences. What if you could invite other people from around the globe to have discussions about those images? What if you and your students could annotate them with your own descriptions and observations? What if you could become a part of a community that contributes images of similar topics for you to consume? And what if you could consume those images via an RSS feed so anytime a new picture was added about a topic you were studying it would automatically come to you?

INTRODUCING FLICKR

That's the potential of Flickr.com, which has become the Web-based digital photography portal of choice, especially since it was purchased by Yahoo in March 2005. To be sure, there are other online sites that offer to host images, but Flickr has evolved into something much more than just a photo publishing space. Personally, I think Flickr is one of the best sites on the Web. It's true social software where the contributors interact and share and learn from each other in creative and interesting ways. And for that reason, its educational potential is huge.

Why consider posting images to the Web in the first place? From a classroom standpoint, think about the ability to capture daily events or highlights and easily share those with parents, community, and colleagues. Field trips, speakers, visitors, special projects, and much more could become a part of any classroom's "photo stream" and could be a great way of sharing the teaching and learning experience. And what better way to celebrate the good work that students do every day than by putting it online for all (or some) to see?

Before we get into the details, however, one disclaimer. As with most other things on the Web, no one can guarantee with absolute certainty the quality or appropriateness of the content on Flickr. Flickr members self-police the photos that are uploaded, and most offensive content is removed from the public access area shortly after it is published. The vast majority of the millions of photos on the site are appropriate for all. That being said, however, take the time to become familiar with the potentials and risks of Flickr before you bring it into your classroom, and make time to convey your expectations and teach appropriate use of the site to your students.

Let's run through the basics first. First, Flickr is free as long as you don't publish more than 20MB of images a month. If you develop some basic editing and file-saving skills to manage file size, this means that you could easily post 100 images a month without too much worry. If you do want to go beyond that, a "Pro" account for $24.95 a year that gives you 10 times the amount of space as well as other features. You need to register with Flickr to publish photos or take part in discussions, and you need a valid e-mail address to do that. If you are thinking of using this with a class of students, you could create one login for all of them to share, or have them create their own accounts. Just follow the pretty standard login procedures from Flickr's homepage.

Once you've set up your account, you're ready to get started. Adding images to your Flickr folder is easy; just click on the upload link, find the image you want to publish, and click "Upload." If you like, you can also upload images using an e-mail function that you set up in the "Your Account" section. Just to be clear, you should do all of your photo editing and adjusting on your computer before you upload your image to Flickr. During the upload process, you can restrict access to what you publish by selecting from three different options. If you opt to restrict viewing access to "Friends" or "Family" for instance, only those people who you have invited as members of those groups will be able to see them. This means that you can work with your students behind closed screens, so to speak, exchanging photos and having conversations that no one else can read or join. From a K–12 standpoint, it's one of the best features of Flickr. Or, of course, you can allow anyone to see and interact with an image by making it "Public."

LEARNING WITH FLICKR

Once you have your photos online, it's time to start creating learning opportunities. One of the most useful tools in Flickr is the annotation feature, which allows you to add notes to parts of the image simply by dragging a box across an area and typing text into a form. Afterwards, when you drag your mouse across the picture, the boxes and annotations pop up.

For example, Sophie, a third grader at Tim Lauer's Lewis Elementary School, used the Flickr annotation tool to help identify the different features of a model she had created of Jane Goodall's camp in Africa (http://flickr.com/photos/lewiselementary/69461520/). (See Figure 7.1.) So when you drag your mouse around the photo, notes pop up that identify what you are looking at, such as Goodall's typewriter, a map Goodall used to plan her expeditions, and the pots and pans Goodall used to cook.

Figure 7.1   Flickr allows you to annotate certain parts of a picture and also provides a way for people to discuss the picture in detail.

A model of Jane Goodall's camp in Africa

Just the uses of this function are pretty compelling. Imagine being able to annotate portions of a Civil War battlefield or a fetal pig dissection for students to access and review. Or as a test of their knowledge, ask them to annotate what they see. Remember, you and your students can use any digital image at your disposal—whether you have taken it or found it on the Web—as long as you attribute the source. (The copyright issues of using an image already found on the Web fall under the Fair Use Doctrine in this instance.) So if you find a photo at the New York Public Library's extensive photo archive that you'd like to work with, you can move it to a private space in Flickr, add a link to the original, and make it a part of your curriculum. In addition, at this writing there are more than 2 million photos posted at Flickr that carry Creative Commons copyright licenses, which allow for their legal reuse in any number of ways (http://flickr.com/creativecommons/). Using Creative Commons licenses, the photographers who publish their own photos to Flickr can indicate what types of uses they will allow for those images. In most instances, these content providers simply ask that the work be attributed to them and that images not be used for commercial purposes.

Another great aspect of Flickr is the ability to start online discussions about the images you post by adding comments under any particular photo. And remember, these conversations can be held in private depending on what level of security you have assigned to your photos. What this means is that you can ask your students to interpret or comment further on what they see, all in the spirit of teaching them how to come to a collaboratively created understanding of a particular image's use or meaning. And, even better, you can subscribe to these discussions via the RSS feed that Flickr creates for your "Recent Comments." That way you can track what your students are writing without having to visit the photo page.

But the real power of Flickr lies in the ways it can connect people from around the world. Each photo that gets uploaded to Flickr can have tags or keywords associated with it by the publisher, and those tags are then searchable. In this way, "public" images of similar themes or topics find each other, and in many cases, so do the people behind them. Some of the most popular tags, as you might guess, are "wedding," "vacation," "family," and "friends." But there's probably a photo for just about every tag you can think of. If your students are studying other countries or cultures, Flickr can be an incredible resource of images and information, and with teacher moderation, there can even be opportunities to meet and learn with other people and students from far-flung places. By leaving a comment on the photos they find, students can potentially learn more about the photographer and the photograph. And again, this can be done in a safe way without students divulging any personal information.

Organizing photos at Flickr is easy because it allows you to create separate albums for different sets of pictures. It even has a slide show function so you can create a series of moving images with just a few clicks of the mouse. Both of these tools can be found by clicking the "Organize" link. So students can create their own personalized collections of photos that they themselves have taken or found on the Web, complete with annotations and discussion with others. Flickr could also serve as a student's online portfolio with digital images of her work that are annotated with reflective descriptions and commented on by peers and mentors. Or what about using Flickr to connect students and teachers during their summer vacations, posting pictures of their travels and talking back and forth about what they are seeing and learning? That's a pretty powerful application if you ask me.

But there's more. Although Flickr is all about putting photos up on the Web, it's also a great resource to use to teach all sorts of other skills and literacies. First of all, there is some really great photography that people are publishing for public consumption and discussion. (For instance, take a look at this slide show of incredibly beautiful plants and flowers: http://flickr.com/groups/secretlife/pool/show/)

Flickr has also proven to be a valuable tool from a current events standpoint. Many times in the past year when major news events have occurred, photos have appeared on Flickr even before large news organization Websites post them. When Hurricane Katrina devastated parts of the Gulf Coast last summer, Flickr became a collection place for many of the on-the-scene photos that people were able to publish. It has become a powerful tool for amateur journalists who use their camera phones to e-mail photos right to their Flickr pages, posting images almost as they happen. (Of course, this is something that you and your students can do as well provided you have the right phone.) There are many ways in which teachers and students can learn about news and photojournalism in this way.

This publishing stream can work two ways as well. Not only is it easy to send pictures to Flickr, but it's also easy to send images from Flickr to your aggregator, Weblog, or Webpage. The most obvious implementation of this is to stream to the class homepage all of the photos your students publish. That way they are collected in an easily accessible space. If students have their own Weblogs, they can add their own photostreams as well. Think, for instance, of a student who is studying, say, clouds. Currently, more than 119,000 photos are tagged "clouds" in Flickr's database, and more are being added nearly every day. Those pictures could be brought right to the blog via the RSS feed for that tag, or via the "Blog This" feature that appears with every photo you can view on the site. Or, at the very least, they could be collected in the student's aggregator (which, by now, I'm sure he has set up!).

FLICKR IN PRACTICE

A number of educators have already started finding creative uses for Flickr in a variety of disciplines. Middle school math teacher James Tubbs from Middletown, Ohio, has been one of the most enthusiastic adopters of the service and has come up with a number of creative applications. On his "7th Grade Math" Weblog (http://verity7math .blogspot.com/), he regularly posts a photo from his Flickr account that either represents a topic his students are studying or a problem they need to solve. They then discuss the assignment in the blog (see Figure 7.2). Tubbs will use photos as writing prompts, journal entries, inquiry projects, and more. His goals are to get his students to write about math more often, to think about the problems they are solving, to spur discussion, assist with assessment, and review prior learning. From the looks of the responses from his students, it seems to be working well (http://misterteacher.blogspot.com/2005/04/linear-patterns-flickr-in-practice.html).

Then there is Steve Brooks, who writes the Edugadget Weblog, where you can find "plain talking technology reviews for teachers" (www.edugadget.com). Brooks especially likes the Creative Commons section of Flickr where teachers can be sure students are using images appropriately.

"The thing I like about getting images from Flickr is the students can see that there are real people behind the images, not some generic, faceless website," writes Brooks on his Weblog. "Real people, like them, have created the pictures, shared them with everyone else, and usually only asked to be credited. There are all kinds of lessons to be taught in those actions" (Brooks, 2005).

Brooks suggests all sorts of activities: For example, "photo field trips," in which students search for images from a certain part of the world from at least three different people and then put them together in a PowerPoint presentation with reflection on what they found. Or "random writes," in which students go to the main screen in the Creative Commons section, type in the first word that comes to mind in the tag field, take the first image in the photostream that comes up, and write a story about it. And, one of my favorites, "Make it Mine," in which students take images from the Creative Commons section, modify and "remix" them on their own computers using a paint or photo editing package, and then republish to Flickr with credit to the work's original owner.

David Jakes is also thinking about ways to use Flickr. Jakes, an educational technology coordinator from Illinois who blogs at "The Strength of Weak Ties" decided to create an imaged version of the poem "Chicago" by Carl Sandburg by linking Flickr photos to the more tag-able words in the poem. So, for instance he took the words "railroads," "stormy," "city," "big shoulders," and others and associated Flickr photos with them.

"I was thinking of all the interpretive possibilities with literature and with the shear volume of photography at Flickr, the endless possibilities to create visual stories with Flickr, that could link Flickr

Figure 7.2 Math teacher James Tubbs uses photos from Flickr as writing prompts and examples of mathematical concepts. (Used with permission of James Tubbs.)

MONDAY, MAY 02, 2005

Roll of the Die

Dados, originally uploaded by A Outra Voz.

In our last short cycle of the year (yeah!), we will be covering probability. The following questions are about the photo above. They will test what you already know about probability.

1) How many possible OUTCOMES are there when tossing a die?

2) What is the THEORETICAL probability of tossing a 1? Write your answer as a fraction.

3) Suppose you toss the die 20 times and a 6 comes up on 3 of those tosses? What is the EXPERIMENTAL probability? Write as a fraction.

4) Suppose you toss the die twice. What is the probability of rolling a 2 both times?

photography with works from authors like Sandburg, or of course, our students," he writes on his blog. "Imagine taking a piece of beautiful photography and a likewise beautiful poem and merging the two together in a 21st Century product . . . *that would be the result of 21st Century open source thinking and learning*" (Jakes, 2005).

MORE FLICKR FUN

People love Flickr so much that there have been a host of creative applications built around it, some of which also have interesting uses in the classroom. "The Great Flickr Tools Collection" (http://pchere .blogspot.com/2005/03/great-flickr-tools-collection.html) is a great place to start. One of my favorites is Geobloggers (www.geoblog gers.com/), which brings together all Flickr photos tagged with latitude and longitude information onto a Google Map for your viewing pleasure. So if you go to Geobloggers and put in the latitude and longitude for say, Washington, DC, up will pop a map that includes links to every photo that's been posted from the area. Imagine your students using this to create a photo tour of your community or city. Very cool.

Or how about the Flickr Color Picker, which will allow you to use a slider to adjust lightness and darkness to show you photos with that main color. Or the FlickrReplacr Bookmarklet (www.kokogiak.com/ flickreplacr.html) that will allow you to highlight a word on any Webpage and swap in a Flickr photo with that tag. Or the Flickr Photostream Bookmarklet that with one click of a button will add any image to your personal archive from any page you might be visiting. It's a great way to easily collect pictures of places or people or whatever your subject might be. Or you can play "Flicktion" by having students pick a random photo from Flickr and write a story about it. Check out the stories already on Flickr at http://flickr.com/ photos/tags/flicktion/. Or . . . well, you get the idea. There's a lot out there to play with and learn.

That is the power of the Read/Write Web: being able to create and connect content through publishing in ways we never thought possible. Flickr is a great tool for introducing students not only to digital images and publishing, but to the social conversations and collaborative learning opportunities that the Web now offers.

Podcasting and Screencasting: Multimedia Publishing for the Masses

Whenever I listen to one of 14-year-old Matthew Bischoff's home-grown radio shows on my iPod, I am always struck by his sense of audience. Even in his first few "podcasts," as they have come to be known, it was obvious that he was a young man who was not speaking to just his friends or family. He was speaking to the unknown thousands of people who started downloading and listening to Matthew's shows in late 2004 when podcasting was born. "This IS Escape From the World" he would half-shout into the microphone, "and I'm your host Matthew Bischoff, a 13-year-old from New Jersey, podcasting from his bedroom." It was, and is, great stuff (Bischoff, 2005).

Matthew was one of the first of what has turned into tens of thousands of people who have taken the easy-publishing meme of the Read/Write Web into the world of multimedia. And it's not just audio. It's video, as in videoblogging, the use of a blog to post video clips of all sorts. And it's video in the form of screencasting as in capturing what happens on a computer screen, adding a bit of audio narrative, and publishing it as multimedia Web tours or stories. And more.

This expansion into multimedia has come about quickly and is fast evolving. This is due primarily to the sudden explosion of broadband connectivity and cheap memory on computers. These days, it doesn't take hours to download a feature length film, a fact that Netflix and Blockbuster are already starting to capitalize on. Similarly, it doesn't take an expensive computer to be able to store and play those files, as hard drive disk space and RAM have become incredibly cheap compared to what they were just a few years ago. Those two advances have created another change in the way we consume multimedia. Whereas our computers used to play the media file as it streamed through the connection, now it simply downloads it and plays it once completely saved. This has made viewing of these types of files much more efficient and enjoyable, and it has pushed streaming of content further into the realm of live performance.

But whatever the technology, the simple fact is that it has become much easier to create and consume multimedia as well as text and digital images. And that has created even more in terms of the potential uses of this new Web that we are dealing with.

PODCASTING

Podcasting is basically the creation and distribution of amateur radio, plain and simple. And it's the distribution piece of this that's important, because although we've been able to do digital audio for some time now, getting a lot of people to listen to it hasn't been very easy. Now it is. Many podcasts are basically normal, everyday people just talking about things that interest them with a bit of music mixed in. Others are more serious and focused in content, offering up the latest interesting news on a particular topic, interviews with interesting people, or recordings of interesting keynotes and presentations.

Whereas Weblog was the word of the year for 2004, I wouldn't at all be surprised to see podcast get the same distinction for 2005. Podcasting is all the rage, and that means, of course, that the barrier to entry is pretty low. Like the other technologies that we've talked about in this book, you do not need a lot of technical expertise to make it work.

Here's what you need to create a basic podcast: a digital audio recorder that can create an MP3 file, some space on a server to host the file, a blog, and something to say. That's it. That's part of the reason why in the first 6 months of its existence, more than 5,000 new podcasts were born, and the number continues to explode. The other part of the quick success of podcasting comes from the fact that, not only are they easy to create, they are easy to consume as well. And that's because of RSS.

Just like it allows people to subscribe to your Weblog, RSS allows people to subscribe to your podcast. And just like new blog content shows up in your aggregator whenever it's posted, new podcasts show up in your MP3 player whenever they are created. Say, for instance, you are subscribed to Matthew Bischoff's "Escape From the World" podcast. Whenever you program it to do so, the free podcast aggregator software that sits on your computer will go out and check to see if Matthew has a new show for you to listen to and, if so, will download it to your computer. Even better, if your MP3 player is connected to your computer at the time, the software will send it over automatically. So, conceivably, you could wake up every morning, disconnect your player from the computer and go out for that early morning run or drive with a whole list of new content to listen to.

Apple loves this, of course, because it's suddenly made the iPod into a mobile radio station that can hold personalized, time-shifted content for your consumption whenever you feel like. And they also love it because of the name. All of this could just as easily be "audiocasting" or "blogcasting" or something else, but podcasting seems to have stuck.

So who is podcasting? Mostly it's people from all different walks of life with all sorts of interests. However, most major news organizations have jumped on the podcast bandwagon with nightly news summaries, special features, and regular shows. One of my favorites in this vein is the "On the Media" show from NPR, which I never got a chance to listen to before they made their podcast version. Politicians are starting to get into the podcasting groove, specifically New York gubernatorial candidate Eliot Spitzer, who started making weekly shows early in 2005, and former senator and vice-presidential candidate John Edwards, both of whom obviously see the genre as way of getting out their respective messages. Businesses, churches, governments, and, you guessed it, schools are getting into the act as well.

The best place to start your podcasting indoctrination is to take some time to listen to a few shows. But be prepared: this is not the highly polished, professional radio you might be used to. Cracks and pops, obscure music, and "ums" and "ahs" are all a part of the podcast genre. Remember, most podcasters are just average Jills and Joes, with day jobs and kids and responsibilities, and ideas that they want to share. Try not to let production value overwhelm what might be really interesting content.

Figure 8.1 iTunes is Apple's free software to help you find podcasts to listen to and to list the shows you create.

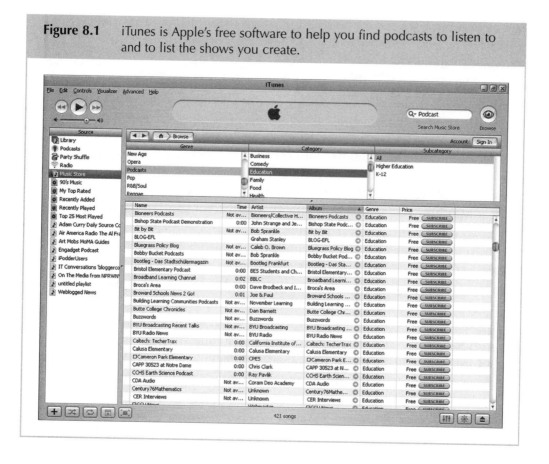

It's no surprise that Apple has incorporated support for listening and subscribing to podcasts into iTunes, its software for managing music on the iPod (see Figure 8.1). In case you're not using an iPod (and there are a lot of great alternatives out there), iTunes is free for download from the Apple site (www.apple.com/itunes/). Once you have it up and running, if you click on the "Podcasts" link from the "Source" list on the left, and then click "Podcast Directory" from the bottom of the main screen, you'll be taken to Apple's complete list of shows at the iTunes store. Here you can search for podcasts, see what's hot and new, and find shows by genre. To find the education-related shows, just click on "Education" in the categories link on the left-hand side of the page. From the next page, you can double-click on a particular show to listen to it, or click the "Subscribe" button to add it to your iTunes list. Then anytime you want iTunes to check if there are any new shows out there, just click the "Update" button in the upper right-hand corner of the page. (For more on the complete

uses of iTunes, see http://ipodlounge.com/index.php/articles/
comments/the-complete-guide-to-itunes-49-with-podcasts/)

If iTunes isn't your cup of tea, you might try the client at indiepodder
.org, where you can find shows about everything from bicycling to
finance to technology to aviation. Or try podcastalley.com, where there
are links to more than 100 education-related shows of varying content
and quality. There you can either listen to the shows as you find them
or save them to your computer for later. Rather than iTunes, you can
start to subscribe to the shows you want by using the iPodder client,
downloadable free from indiepodder.org. Save the file to your computer and then double-click it to go through the setup process. Once
you have iPodder up and running, you take the RSS feeds from the
shows you want to listen to (remember how to do that?) and paste
them into the "Add Feed Manually" form. Then, click the "Scheduler"
tab and set the time of day you want your computer to search for any
new podcasts and download them automatically.

Once you have the aggregator set up, you need one more step to
get your podcasts loaded directly to your MP3 player. For those of you
that have iPods, you can use iTunes. If you leave your iPod docked
and plugged into the computer at night, iPodder and iTunes will do
everything you need to make any new podcasts available for listening
in the morning. If you don't have an iPod, you might need to use
Windows Media Player to move your files around. Open Media Player
and click on "Tools" then "Options," and then select the "Library" tab.
From there, click the "Monitor Folders" button and "Add" the folder
where iPodder stores the podcasts you are subscribed to, usually C:\
Documents and Settings\your user name\Application Data\
iPodder\downloads (for a more detailed description of how to do
this, see Jake Luddington's post on "Podcasting with Windows Media
Player," www.jakeludington.com/archives/000405.html). Then, plug
in your MP3 player and use the "Sync" tab to drag and drop the files
you want.

PODCASTS AND SCHOOLS

As with most of these other technologies, it's not hard to see how
podcasts might make inroads in schools. One way to get into the flow
of education-related podcasting is to visit the Education Podcast
Network (http://epnweb.org/), which was started in May 2005. Not
only is there a growing directory of educators who are doing personal
podcasts, there are links to suggested classroom uses broken down
both by grade level and subject.

And remember that the underlying technology here is digital recording and the idea that it is now *very easy* to create and publish these recordings. You and your students may not have iPods or MP3 players, and the good news is you don't need them to start using audio in this way. As long as you have a way to make the recording, and as long as your students have access to the Internet, you can make this work. More about that in a minute.

In general, radio broadcasting is now a reality for the vast majority of schools that can't afford radio stations. About $100 and an Internet connection is all you need to start doing regular radio shows with your students. And once again, the motivating factor, to me at least, is that the content of these shows does not have to be limited to a school or community audience. Podcasting is yet another way for them to be creating and contributing ideas to a larger conversation, and it's a way of archiving that contribution for future audiences to use.

Take George Mayo, for instance. He's a first-year teacher in Virginia who last year started a Weblog magazine with his students called M&M Online Magazine (http://mrmayo.typepad.com/magazine/). When his students got the hang of that form of Web publishing, they decided to add an accompanying podcast that was written and produced by the class (http://mrmayo.typepad.com/podcasts/). They created their own intro music using Apple's Garageband software, and in the podcast itself they discuss what's new in the magazine, which is a collection of individually run student blogs.

Another example is Radio WillowWeb from the Willowdale Elementary School in Omaha, Nebraska (www.mpsomaha.org/willow/radio/index.html). As the Website says, these Willowcasts are "online radio shows for kids by kids" (site shown in Figure 8.2). Each show has its own host, theme, and unique segments, which can include things such as "Bad Joke, Good Joke," "Holiday Spotlight," "Poetry Corner," and much more. It's a great example of what you can do with podcasts.

Bob Sprankle, a third- and fourth-grade teacher at Wells Elementary in Wells, Maine, moderates Bob Sprankle's Room 208 podcast (http://bobsprankle.com/blog/). Aside from weekly shows that cover events at school, his students have done "sound-seeing tours" of the local Willowbrook Museum Village in Newfield that they visited on a field trip. Listeners are treated to the students' reactions to what they see, the presentations by the tour guides, and all sorts of other vignettes of students talking and thinking about what they're seeing, sometimes with teacher prompts. It's a concept that's easy to replicate.

Finally, there is the Lincoln (NE) Southwest High School podcasts that are hosted by teacher Dennis Hershberger and feature reports by

Figure 8.2   Students at Willowdale Elementary in Nebraska are podcasting about their school on a regular basis. (Used with permission of Tony Vincent.)

students on upcoming events, interviews, reviews, and whatever else might be of interest (http://lsw.lps.org/dhersh/podcast.html). All of these shows are great examples of how teachers might easily integrate amateur radio into the classroom.

But podcasting doesn't have to be just edu-radio. There are many other ways that teachers could bring the genre into the classroom. World language teachers could record and publish daily practice lessons that students could listen to at home or, if they are fortunate enough, could download to their own MP3 players. Like the Madrid Young Learners Podcasts (http://mylcpodcasts.blogspot.com/) site where an English speaker tells a story via a podcast and non-English-speaking listeners answer questions in English via comments. How hard would it be to make your own site like this (now that you know how to blog) with teachers enlisting native speakers from around the world to tell stories that their own students respond to?

Social studies teachers could have their students do oral histories or interviews or reenactments of historical events. Science teachers could have students narrate labs or dissections or experiments to record their processes. Music teachers could record weekly recitals or special events as podcasts. All teachers could record important parts of what they do in the classroom that can then be archived to the class Weblog and used by students who may have missed the class or just want a refresher on what happened.

Steve Brooks over at EduGadget.com has some suggestions that schools and districts might want to think about, including guided "pod-tours" of the campus on back-to-school night (perhaps created by students), or tours of art displays narrated by the artists. You could record assemblies, do new teacher orientations, have supervisors record descriptions of their departments, and record board meetings for students, teachers, and parents who are unable to attend. Principals could record weekly or monthly messages to community or teachers or even students. As with blogs, the possibilities are only limited by your imagination (Brooks, 2005).

Apple offers up some ideas of its own of how iPods can be used in the classroom, and they come complete with lesson plans and samples (www.apple.com/education/ipod/lessons/). Currently the list includes ideas about learning math with music, iPod reporting, audio travel albums, and many more.

Remember, all of these ideas can be put into practice simply by recording digital audio, but the key to turning your or your student recordings into podcasts is to publish them. That's what the Read/Write Web is all about: being able to share what you create with others. As I've said before, keep thinking about ways to add these student contributions to the larger database of learning that's out there.

GETTING STARTED WITH PODCASTING

Before you get your students podcasting, I would urge you to try it out first. Again, I think you need to experience what you are asking your students to do not only so you can support their technical use, but also so you understand what Web publishing really feels like. Although the following may seem a bit high-end technically, podcasting is one of those technologies that can be as simple or as complex as you want it to be. And like all of these technologies, once you've done it a couple of times, it should come pretty easily.

First, you need a way to record digital audio. You can do this a couple of different ways, by plugging a microphone into your computer to record, or by recording directly onto some MP3 players. (Some handheld devices and mobile phones also make this possible.) iPods, for instance, have microphone attachments that allow you to record directly to your iPod in MP3 format. These are great for doing mobile recordings, like on field trips or while driving (not recommended). Take some time to experiment, record, and listen to see what kind of quality you can get and whether or not it suits your needs. And you'll also need to learn how to get the recordings off of your player and onto your computer. Depending on what type of portable recorder you use, you can use iTunes or Windows Media Player to do this when you attach your player.

Making MP3 recordings on your computer is pretty easy and inexpensive as well, and generally the quality is better. In addition, you save the step of having to transfer your recording over from your handheld device. You'll need some software to capture what you record in MP3 format, and I would recommend the open-source program Audacity (http://audacity.sourceforge.net/), which is free, easy to use, and a good audio-editing program as well. (You'll also need to download Audacity's MP3 encoder at http://audacity.sourceforge.net/help/faq?s=install&item=lame-mp3 separately to translate your files into MP3s.) Remember that if you use Audacity, you need to choose "Export as MP3" under the file menu when you've finished recording and editing. And remember, too, that you can use Audacity to clean up the recordings you create on your MP3 players (see Figure 8.3 for an image of Audacity).

One other way to capture audio content for podcast is to us the free Internet telephone service Skype (www.skype.com) to record interviews with people from around the world. (The only requirement is that they have Skype too.) In fact, you can hold and record conference calls of up to five people. You'll need the free Skype recording add on from PowerGramo (www.powergramo.com) as well. And a headset microphone would really improve the quality. Just download the software, set up your Skype account, get the Skype names of the other people you want to talk to, record the phone call, and use Audacity to export it as an MP3. Personally, I think there is huge potential for using Skype in this way in the classroom.

Once you have your "studio" ready, you need to figure out what you want to do or say for your test run. Maybe, as many pioneer edu-podcasters like Steve Dembo (teach42.com) or David Warlick (davidwarlick.com) or Steve Sloan (edupodder.com) are wont to do, you can share your ideas about where education is headed or what's the latest news in schools. Or perhaps you want to create an audio tour of your classroom, interview some other teachers, recite poetry, or even sing a little bit (in my case, a very little bit). Whatever you decide to do, think about your audience, because you'll be asking your students to do the same. (You may even want to write out your first few podcasts beforehand, but I would urge you to try not to read from a prepared script.)

Figure 8.3   Audacity is a free, open-source program that makes it easy to edit and mix your audio files. (Used with permission of Audacity. See p. 138 for an enlarged screenshot.)

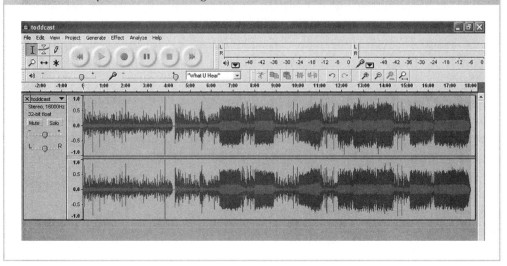

If you're using Audacity to record onto your computer, just plug your microphone in and click on the "Record" button. Don't worry too much about fooling around with the levels and the settings to start. Just make some short recordings and play them back to see how they sound. If you have a microphone attachment and are using your MP3 player as a recorder, you'll need to go through the synching up process for whatever player you have to get the recorded files onto your hard drive.

When you've finished the talking part of your podcast, you might want to do a little editing and production. Using Audacity, you can easily edit out all of the "ums" and "ahs," unless of course you find they add charm to your show. (Not to jump ahead, but there is a great video/audio screencast by Matt Pasiewicz on using Audacity at www.educause.edu/Screencasts/Audacity/Untitled.html.) Even better, you can use Audacity to add intro or transition music to your work. If you have the means to create your own digital music, GarageBand for instance, you don't have to worry about the copyright issues of using other people's work. If you can't make your own, you might surf on over to Wikimedia Commons (http://commons.wikimedia.org/wiki/Main_Page) to find some free-use music that's legal to add.

Here's how: After you have saved the files to your computer, use the "Import Audio" feature under the Project section in Audacity to start editing and mixing. Start with your own recording. Press the play button to start listening, and then use the "Selection Tool" (the icon that looks like an *I* in the upper left-hand corner) to drag over the parts of the file that you want to edit out, and hit delete. When you've finished with that, import your music track the same way and then line up the timing between the tracks by using the "Time Shift Tool" (the one that looks like a two-headed arrow). You can fade one track in by using the Selection Tool and then choosing "Fade In" from the Effects section. It may look daunting, but if you play just a little, you should be able to do some editing and production in no time. Or not: Remember, one of the charms of podcasting is its unfinished quality. So don't get worn down by production if it doesn't suit you. When you're done, just "Export as MP" from the File section, and you're ready to publish.

The first step to sharing your podcast is to transfer the MP3 file you made from your computer to a server that's on the Internet. If you have a Web server at your school, that's probably your best bet. (In this case, maybe your first podcast should be one that highlights the fine work of your school's Webmaster.) But even if you don't, or even if you for some reason can't use that server, there are alternatives. The first is OurMedia.org, which "provides free storage and free band-width for your videos, audio files, photos, text or software. Forever. No catches." Just sign up for a free account and upload your MP3 using their easy process. Wherever you put it, you use the unique URL that is assigned to the file to create a direct link to it in your blog or Website. When people click the link, they'll hear your creation.

The other way to get your file on the Internet is through the blog software that you use. Most of the popular blog software such as Movable Type, WordPress, and Manila now have automatic support for "enclosures" like MP3s (or any other type of file for that matter). When you create the post that describes your podcast, you'll be able to add the MP3 file to the post automatically by attaching it. (This process varies depending on your software . . . search for "enclo-sures" in the Help.) This step gets the file onto a server and automat-ically links it in your post. And, in this case, it means that people (students) who want to listen to the audiocasts you've created can do so by simply subscribing to the RSS feed of your blog.

But how can people "subscribe" to your podcasts if you're using Blogger, which doesn't have built-in support for enclosures? One solution is to go to Feedburner.com and create a separate RSS feed for your audience to use. Again, it's not hard to do. At the Feedburner homepage, just paste in the address of your blog into the form and click "Next." On the page that comes up, just scroll down to the "Additional Services" section and select the "SmartCast" option. At the bottom of the page, click "Next" again. You'll be asked to create an account by providing a username and password. On the next page, it will confirm your new feed, which you should then copy and "Activate." Finally, go back to your Blogger blog and create a link to that feed address. Whenever you add a link to an MP3 at your blog, the feed will automatically include it.

If the podcasting bug bites hard and you start creating regular "shows," don't forget to go to the various directories to get yourself listed. Start with iTunes, but Podcastalley.com, Podcastcentral.com, and Podcast.net are a few you might want to go to as well. And with that, you and your students should be well on your way to fame and, well, fame in amateur radio.

SCREENCASTING

One step up from podcasting is screencasting, which is a relatively new medium that I think has a lot of promise in the classroom. Simply put, screencasting involves capturing what you or your students do on the computer with an audio narration to go with it. The easiest way to understand screencasting is to watch one. So, right now, go watch this screencast about Wikipedia that was done by John Udell at http://weblog.infoworld.com/udell/gems/umlaut.html. I'll wait until you come back.

Ok, get the picture? (And "get" Wikipedia a bit more?) The potential is pretty obvious, I think. From a teaching standpoint, you could create screencasts as support materials when teaching complex skills on the computer. If you had a Tablet PC, you could capture the ink annotations or written solutions that you share with your students. You could create training videos for peers, narrate PowerPoint-created tours for parents, or make video collections of exemplary student work. Once again, the possibilities are enormous. (Myscreencast.com is another place you might want to check for examples of the medium.)

With your students, you could ask them to annotate their work in voice as they show it on screen. Or, you could have them create their own Internet tours. Or, have them read stories or poetry they write with accompanying visuals they have either created or found. They can even take some of those podcast ideas and attach visual images to go along with it. It's limited only by your and their creativity.

The best part? It's so easy to do. If you can podcast, you can screencast. But, obviously, screencasting takes a bit more preparation. You're combining audio with video, which means you need to think more carefully about what you want to do and how best to do it. You'll need to prepare what it is you want to show on the computer and you'll probably want to create at least an outline of a script. You might even want to create a storyboard that sketches out the visual and the audio together. No matter how you plan, it's not a bad idea to run through it a couple of times before actually starting to create the screencast.

Unlike blogs and wikis and RSS, this is, however, one of the few tools that works differently depending on operating system. So, to start, let's look at how to make it happen in Windows.

Basically, Windows Media Encoder and a microphone are all you need in a Windows environment. You can download the software free at Microsoft.com (www.microsoft.com/windows/windowsmedia/9series/encoder/default.aspx). They have some good tutorials at the site that you might want to take a look at as well. Save the file to your computer and then double-click it to run the installation. (Again, if you have restrictions on loading software to your computer, you may need to get some technical assistance.)

Once you've plugged in your microphone, open up Encoder. At the "New Session" dialogue box, select the "Capture Screen" option (see Figure 8.4). Remember that if you decide to capture the entire screen, the file resulting file size will be bigger. If you can just capture a portion of the screen, try to do so. (You can also keep the file size down by lowering your screen resolution and color depth; just right-click anywhere on the desktop and then select Properties and then Settings.) Make sure to check the "Capture Audio from Default Audio Device" box. (NOTE: You have to remember to do this every time to you start another recording.)

If you chose to capture just a region of the screen, you'll be asked to define your selection box. Click the selection button and drag over the area you want to grab. To see the border while you go through your screens, click on the "Flash border during capture" box. If you chose to capture the entire screen, your next step is to create a file name and tell the computer where you want to save it. Obviously, make sure you remember the spot. Then, select the quality you want the screencast to be. As always this is a choice between file size and viewing. I almost always opt for larger files and better video by choosing "High." Finally, Encoder asks you to provide some information about the screencast that will be attached to the final product. This step is optional. Click "Finish" to, well, finish the setup.

When you're ready, click the "Start Encoding" button at the top of the dialogue box. The box will disappear, and you can start moving through your screens and doing the voice narration. When you're done, just click on the Encoder tab from your program tray, which automatically pauses the capture, and then click "Stop." You'll be given the option of previewing what you just did and then saving it. I'd urge you

Figure 8.4   You can use Windows Media Encoder to create videos of what you do on your computer. (Reprinted by permission from Microsoft Corporation.)

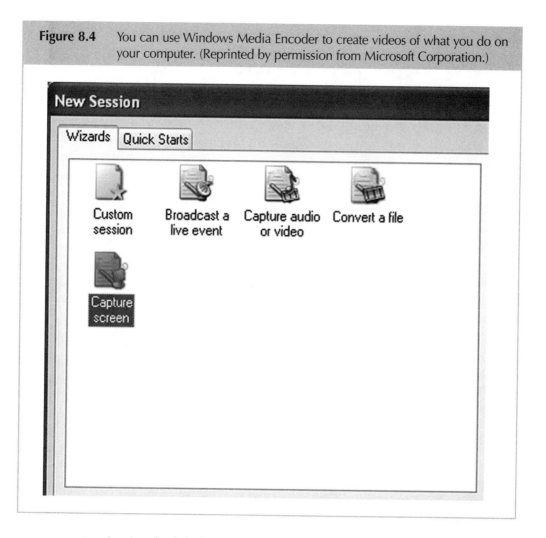

to give it a look before you save. (As a final step, you can use Movie Maker, which comes with Windows XP, to edit your screencast.)

Unfortunately, at this writing, there is no way to do screencasts easily on a Mac for free. One fairly inexpensive option is Snapz Pro (www.ambrosiasw.com/utilities/snapzprox/), which goes for $69. Just open the program, drag a box around the area you want to capture, select to record the microphone track, go through your screencast, and just click save. Really, it's that easy. Snapz Pro creates a Quick Time movie that works on either platform if you have the software.

When you're all finished, you can publish your work much the same way you would publish your podcast. OurMedia.org works for video, too. And if you or your students start creating regular podcasts, make sure you add the feed to the directories at iTunes or iPodder or the rest. In case you've forgotten, publishing to an audience can be a great motivator for students. Podcasting and screencasting are another great way of getting student content online.

9 What It All Means

S o now that you have a good idea of the tools and the pedagogies, what is going to be the impact on education? Obviously, that's a huge question, but it's important to try to put some meaning to the message.

No doubt, the classroom of the Read/Write Web is going to be defined by two unstoppable trends in the use of these technologies. First, with more than 10 billion pages already on the Web, more and more content both new and old will continue to come online. If you don't believe that, witness the announcement by Google that it plans to scan and digitize more than 50 million books from five of the largest research libraries from around the world. In the words of New York Public Library CEO Paul LeClerc, that in itself "is one of the most transformative events in the history of information distribution since Gutenberg" (Graham, 2004). Add to that the desire of Internet Archive.org founder Brewster Kahle's wish to do the same to the 500 million volumes in the Library of Congress and there is little doubt that the Internet will continue to explode as the most comprehensive source of information in history. As author Thomas Friedman writes in *The World Is Flat: A Brief History of the Twenty-first Century*, "we are now in the process of connecting all of the knowledge pools in the world together" (Friedman, 2005). There's no doubt that the ability of our teachers and students to use that knowledge effectively is of the highest importance.

The second trend is that, more and more, the creation of that content is collaborative. Just about every major software package on the market these days has collaborative tools built in; witness the "Shared Workspace" features of Microsoft Office software that allow teams of people to share and develop documents, presentations, and spreadsheets to name a few. And the open-source development of operating systems such as Linux or browsers like Mozilla's Foxfire is setting a model for collaboration that more and more businesses and even schools are tapping into.

When today's students enter their post-education professional lives, odds are pretty good that they will be asked to work with others collaboratively to create content for diverse and wide-ranging audiences. Compare that to an educational system that, by and large, asks those same students to work independently for a very narrow audience (usually the teacher who gives the grade) and the disconnect becomes painfully clear.

Right now, teachers are employing Weblogs and wikis and the like in ways that are transforming the curriculum and are allowing learning to continue long after the class ends. They are tapping into the potential of a World Wide Web that is a conversation, not a lecture, where knowledge is shaped and acquired through a social process, and where ideas are presented as a starting point for dialogue, not an ending point (Siemens, 2005). In case after case, the walls of the classroom are literally made irrelevant by the creation of communities of learners that span oceans, races, genders, and generations.

NEW LITERACIES

In the age of the Read/Write Web, the explosion of information and online technologies demands a more complex definition of what it means to be literate. For more than a hundred years we have defined being literate as being able to read and to write. And although those core abilities are still central to learning, they are no longer enough to ensure understanding.

First, due in large measure to the ease with which people can now publish to the Internet, consumers of Web content need to be editors as well as readers. Print sources have always carried with them the assumption that the content included had been reviewed or checked before published. Books, newspapers, and magazines all have editors whose job it is to make sure the information is verifiably accurate. But today, anyone with an Internet connection can now publish without any prior review. Although this is good in terms of creating a wider body of knowledge to draw from, it obviously requires that we teach our students to become more active consumers of that information instead of just passively accepting it as legitimate. Editing, then, means being a critical reader and viewer, not simply accepting what is presented.

Second, to truly take advantage of the power of the Read/Write Web, we must be literate in the ways of publishing. In many ways, we now truly have a free press that the framers of the Constitution envisioned, where everyone can have a voice. We must then teach and model the ways in which ideas and products can be brought online.

Third, in the process, we need to have the ability to work closely with others in virtual environments. Within that collaborative model are literacies regarding communication skills and process.

Finally, we need to know how to manage the information that we consume. Our students will be required to collect, store, and retrieve relevant information throughout their lives, and we need to give them the skills to do so effectively and efficiently. Throughout this book, we have looked at how the tools can support these literacies.

THE BIG SHIFTS

So, the classroom of the Read/Write Web is one of seamless transfer of information; of collaborative, individualized learning; and of active participation by all members of class. It is marked by the continuous process of creating and sharing content with wide audiences. In many ways, these technologies are demanding that we reexamine the way we think about content and curriculum, and they are nurturing new, important shifts in how best to teach students.

Big Shift #1: Open Content

It used to be that schools and teachers "owned" the content they taught in their classrooms. Most curriculum was taught from a textbook with a few added resources copied from various sources thrown in. Perhaps there was a filmstrip (remember those?) or a video that added to the discussion. Outside of what schools provided, however, students had limited access to additional information about the subjects they were studying. There were newspapers and magazines, and there were books in the school and public libraries, but all of these resources required more time and effort to find and consume than the average student wanted to expend.

Today, however, that information is as far away as a Google search, and the breadth and depth of content are staggering. The information students can access is more current as well, rendering many textbooks passé. In fact, many teachers and students have begun writing their own textbooks online using the collaborative spaces now available to them, cobbling together links and annotated reading lists that future classes can build on as well.

More and more, the "code" to teaching and learning that schools once held dear is disappearing, creating open-source-type classrooms in which everyone contributes to the curriculum. This openness leads to the next Big Shift.

Big Shift #2: Many, Many Teachers, and 24/7 Learning

As our access to content increases, so does our access to other teachers. Many other teachers, in fact. The Read/Write Web allows us to connect to not just other Science, or English or Social Studies teachers, however. Instead, we can now find biochemists, scholars of Faulkner, and Civil War reenactors to bring into the classroom. Teachers who harness the potential of these tools are tapping into the knowledge of primary sources such as authors and historians and researchers. And the asynchronous nature of these tools, the ability to interact with content when it's most convenient to do so, means that learning can take place anytime we're ready for it.

As I've said, in my four years as a blogger, I have found hundreds of teachers, people who through their willingness to share their ideas and experiences have informed my practice and my thinking. The rich diversity of cultures, geography, and professional expertise that these sources provide have dramatically broadened my understanding of my own teaching and education in general. Without question, it has been the most extensive and effective learning experience of my life.

But unlike the traditional student–teacher relationship, the student no longer just consumes the content provided by the teachers. Through my Weblog, I am able to be a part of the conversation and, in turn, perhaps teach my teachers through my reflections and ideas. This creates an opportunity for Big Shift #3.

Big Shift #3: The Social, Collaborative Construction of Meaningful Knowledge

For generations, the typical expectation of our students has been that they work independently ("do your own work") and produce that work or content for a limited audience, usually just the teacher giving the grade and perhaps the other students in the class. The work, once it was finished, was exactly that . . . finished. Think of how few opportunities there were for anyone outside the classroom walls to "read" those efforts, whether they were essays or experiments or projects or performances. Think of how much of student work today simply ends up in the recycling bin at the end of the year.

Today, however, the Read/Write Web makes it easy for students to produce work in truly collaborative ways for large audiences. That work can have real purpose and real meaning for the audience that reads and consumes it. Information created and published in this way takes on a new social context that requires us to change the way we think about what we ask our students to produce, not as something to be "finished" but as something to be added to and refined by those outside the classroom who may interact with it.

So, this idea that we can continue to interact with our ideas in collaborative ways leads to the next Big Shift.

Big Shift #4: Teaching Is Conversation, Not Lecture

By publishing content to a wide audience, we say "these are my ideas, my understandings of the world." That in itself is empowering, and with it comes an expectation that our voices will be heard. On their own, our students are learning that their voices matter, that people are listening and responding, and that their ideas count. To not embrace those feelings by continuing to look at curriculum-as-lecture is to fight against a tide that we will not be able to keep back.

As George Siemens says, "Ideas are presented as the starting point for dialogue, not the ending point" (Siemens, 2002). That is the new expectation of the Read/Write Web. To remain relevant, educators are going to have to respond accordingly. By inviting students to become active participants in the design of their own learning, we teach them how to be active participants in their lives and future careers.

This shift from lecture to conversation requires the next Big Shift.

Big Shift #5: Know "Where" Learning

In the Read/Write Web classroom, it's not as essential to know what the answer is as it is to know where to find it. In the past, when information was not as accessible, it was important to memorize facts and formulas. Today, however, factual answers are only a few clicks away. Take for instance the Q & A service that Google instituted in April of 2005 (http://answers.google.com/answers/). Type in a question, and up pops an answer.

Knowing "where" learning also means knowing where to find those good teachers mentioned above. As we move away from textbooks and more "closed" sources of information, we need to be able to create our own texts from many different content providers such as Weblogs, wikis, Websites, discussion groups, and more. So teachers and students have to understand and be able to employ the many different ways to find information on the Web.

And, obviously, it's not enough simply to find these sources. We must be able to identify which of the sources we do find are worthy of our attention. To do so, we need to accept the next Big Shift.

Big Shift #6: Readers Are No Longer Just Readers

In an era of textbooks and printed resources, we could be pretty sure that the content we consumed had been checked and edited before being published. Reading, for all intents, was a fairly passive experience. Today, however, readers cannot assume that what they are reading has been reviewed by someone else with an eye toward truth and accuracy. The Web is now a printing press for the masses, and so readers themselves must learn to be critical consumers of the information they consider. They must be editors with all of the information literacy skills they need to discern good information from bad.

And now given the opportunity to converse and interact with the sources they find, readers must also be writers. We must be able to engage those sources in debate and discussion as one way of assessing their worth.

In all these ways, reading is becoming a more active undertaking, no longer neatly compartmentalized in books and handouts. There is valuable knowledge to be found in thousands, maybe millions of places, which leads us to Big Shift #7.

Big Shift #7: The Web as Notebook

As the Web becomes more and more of a source of content for our teaching and learning, it also renders paper less and less effective as a way to capture the information we find relevant. Hence the Read/*Write* Web. Weblogs and wikis and the like were borne out of the need to save and organize the digital ideas we find interesting so that we can annotate them with our own interpretations and easily return to them when we need to.

And not only can we collect links and text in our Web notebooks, we can include audio, video, photography, and more. In fact, many educators see the Web as the perfect home for electronic learner portfolios that can be shared easily with audiences of peers and mentors. To make that happen, we have to accept Big Shift #8.

Big Shift #8: Writing Is No Longer Limited to Text

As we move away from plain text on the page, we move toward a totally new definition of what it means to write. Certainly, in the short term at least, it remains crucially important to be able to express oneself in writing using words. But it is hard to deny that more and more we have become a multimedia society, relying heavily on television to communicate the important ideas of our culture. According to a study by the National Endowment for the Arts in 2004, fewer than half of American adults now read literature (National Endowment for the Arts, 2004) and that number continues to decline.

But today the technologies of the Read/Write Web allow us to write in many different genres. We can write in audio and video, in music, and in digital photographs, and even in code such as JavaScript, and we can publish all of it easily for extended audiences. As blogger Alan Levine and others say, we can combine many of these forms of writing into a process of "Rip, Mix, and Learn," taking a piece of content here and another piece there, combining it to produce powerful text and nontext messages and interpretations (Levine, 2004).

These genres of writing expand the ways in which we can prove our knowledge and lead us to the next Big Shift.

Big Shift #9: Mastery Is the Product, Not the Test

The Age of the Read/Write Web is an age not only of participation but of production. Think about the limited ways in which we could show mastery in the "old" days. For the vast majority, mastery was exhibited by passing the test. When you think about it, schools are one of the very few places where someone is said to have "mastered" a subject by getting 70% of the test correct. And most of the tests were not based on what you could do with the information. Would you feel safe in a world where kids were awarded drivers licenses by just passing the written test? I didn't think so.

Today, however, students can display mastery in countless ways that involve the creation of digital content for large audiences. Even more traditional forms of showing mastery through performance or putting together projects can now be easily published to the Web in a variety of ways. More and more, the concept of a cheap, accessible, electronic online portfolio is coming to fruition. Leading to the next Big Shift.

Big Shift #10: Contribution, Not Completion, as the Ultimate Goal

All of these technologies allow students and teachers to contribute their own ideas and work to the larger body of knowledge that is the Web. Instead of simply handing in countless assignments to teachers to be read, graded, handed back, and most likely thrown away, we can now offer our students a totally new way of looking at the work they do. It's not meant for the teacher or the class or even the school. It's meant for the world, literally. It's not meant to be discarded or stored in a folder somewhere; it's meant to be added to the conversation and potentially used to teach others.

Obviously, these changes create all sorts of challenges for educators, challenges to the educational system as a whole, and challenges to the traditional roles of teachers in the classroom. First, the educational system itself will be under pressure to respond to the ability of students to learn 24/7 from a variety of sources. The neatly organized four- or eight-period day, 180-day school year may no longer be the most effective structure to teach students in a world filled with easy access to information. The vertical model of a teacher disseminating information and knowledge to students may not be very effective in an environment in which learning is a much more horizontal or collaborative undertaking. But those types of systemic changes will be a long time in coming.

More important will be the response of classroom teachers, for the classroom of the Read/Write Web will in many ways require a redefinition of what it means to teach.

First, teachers will have to start to see themselves as *connectors*, not only of content, but of people. Once again, the access to much greater amounts and more timely information means that it will be imperative for educators to model strategies to not only find worthwhile and relevant content, but to use primary sources in the classroom. We can invite people from around the world to engage in discussions and even content creation with our students, and our teachers must be willing and able to find and use these sources effectively.

Second, teachers must become *content creators* as well. To teach these technologies effectively, educators must learn to use them effectively. They need to become bloggers and podcasters, to use wikis and the other social tools at their disposal. Just like anyone else trying to learn a new language, educators must practice the words, or in this case, the tools. Chris Dede of the Graduate School of Education at Harvard says, "Teachers who use interactive media professionally will find they rapidly develop learning styles and strengths similar to those of their students" (Thatcher, 2005). And they might even come to enjoy it.

Connecting and contributing are not enough, however. Teachers also need to become true *collaborators*. And not just with each other, but with their students as well. For all of the reasons I've previously cited, teachers must begin to see themselves more as learners alongside their students. The New 'Net allows us to tap into the creativity and knowledge of thousands if not millions of teachers and students, and we have to be willing to learn together, both in the classroom and online, to effectively give our students the most relevant experience we can. We can't pretend to know everything any more, and we can't be effective if we don't tap into the work of others who are willing to contribute their ideas and content as well.

Fourth, teachers need to think of themselves more as *coaches* who model the skills that students need to be successful and motivate them to strive for excellence. Ultimately, players on the field take responsibility for their own performance, and they learn through practice and reflection. That needs to be true of students now as well. We teach students the skills of the Read/Write Web and motivate them to seek their own truths and their own learning.

Finally, teachers who use the tools of the Read/Write Web need to be *change agents*. The ideas will not be easily embraced or readily supported at first because of the transparency that they create. So teachers need to find ways to use these tools to move away from the more traditional paradigms of instruction on their own terms in their own ways and recruit others to follow suit.

JUST THE BEGINNING

We are at the beginning of a radically different relationship with the Internet, one that has long-standing implications for educators and students. The coming years will be marked by a flood of new innovation and ideas in teaching, most born from the idea that we can now publish and interact in ways never before possible. In reality, we now have a Read/Reflect/Write/Participate Web, one that will continue to evolve and grow in ways not yet thought of, spurred by the efforts of creative teachers who recognize the potential to improve student learning.

If you have come this far, I'm hoping you have a new box of tools and techniques to take full advantage of the opportunities this new Internet presents. Here is where the real learning, and the real fun, begins.

Epilogue: The Classroom of the Read/Write Web

English teacher Tom McHale sets down his cup of coffee and boots up the computer at his classroom desk. It's 6:50 A.M., and he has about 45 minutes before his sleepy journalism students will begin filing into his classroom. He logs in and opens up his personal Weblog on the school intranet. There, he does a quick scan of the *New York Times* headlines that are displayed on his homepage and clicks on one of the links to read a story about war reporting that he thinks his student journalists might be interested in. With a quick click, Tom uses the "Furl It" button on his toolbar, adds a bit of annotation to the form that comes up, and saves it in his Furl.net journalism folder. With this one step, he archives the page for future reference and automatically sends the link and his note to display on his journalism class portal for students to read when they log in.

Next, he scans a compiled list of summaries that links to all the work his students submitted to their Weblogs the night before. Seeing one particularly well done response, he clicks through to the student's personal site and leaves a positive comment about her submission. (He notices that a couple of his students have already left some positive feedback to the author as well.) He also "Furls" that site, putting it in the "Best Practices" folder, which will send it to the class homepage as well for students to read and discuss, and to a separate Weblog page he has created to keep track of all of the best examples of student work. It's 7:00.

After taking a sip of his coffee, Tom takes a look at his research feeds. He's been asked to keep abreast of the latest news about technology and teaching writing, and this morning he sees his Google search feed has turned up a new version of Write Outloud. He clicks the link, reads about the new version on the site, and then clicks on a different "Furl It" button that uses an account set up for all of his department colleagues to share. When the form comes up, he writes a couple of lines of description about how it might benefit the department, and then saves it in the "Technology" folder, which automatically archives it to the tech page of the English Department Weblog. Later that day, all the members of his department will see his link as well as any others his colleagues may have added as a part of their daily e-mail update from Furl. He also decides he wants to create another search feed for the words "journalism" and "Weblogs." With a click on the toolbar, a dialog box appears and he enters his terms, and then clicks on the Feedster.com radio button (one among four choices). He hits ok, and a new feed headline box is added to his portal.

At around 7:05, Tom uses his personal Weblog to upload an assignment on symbolism for his major American literature class. When he opens up the document online to check it, he adds that to a different Furl folder under his English login, and it gets sent to a separate Web page set up on the English site for American Literature Best Practices. The rest of the American Lit teachers will get an automatic e-mail later in the day notifying them of his published artifact that they can use in their own classes. Then, he creates a post for his Lit class portal that has a link to the assignment, and he publishes the post to the class homepage. Automatically, parents who have requested notification will get an e-mail that their son or daughter has homework to do that evening. E-mails also get sent to a couple of counselors who are tracking at-risk students.

At about 7:15, Tom decides to scan the latest school news feed, which aggregates all the new posts from the school Weblogs he is subscribed to. He sees that the basketball team won the county tournament, the new edition of the school paper is online, and the superintendent has posted important information about an upcoming safety drill. He clicks through to read the entire post, and then leaves a comment suggesting a way to alleviate crowding in the hallways during the drill. (He sees a parent also has a suggestion about the timing.) Back at his page, he decides that he doesn't want to scan the soccer team news any longer, so he goes to his subscription page and unchecks the feed. He does notice, however, the "New Feeds" section lists a new "Tech Deals" feed that the tech supervisor has created. Because he's looking for a new home computer, he clicks to subscribe to it.

At 7:25, he checks his audio library and sees that the MP3 interview that two of his students did with the principal has been downloaded to his player. He lifts it out of its cradle and puts it in his briefcase so he can play it on his car stereo during his ride home after school. If it's good, he'll upload it to the school podcast page, where 135-odd sub-scribers (mostly parents) will automatically receive it so they can hear it and hopefully get most of their questions about the new building project answered.

With just a few minutes left before his first class, Tom opens the personal journal part of his portal and types in a few notes about an idea he had for the lit project his students are completing next week. He files them into the "Literature" subfolder so that he can pull up relevant notes all at once if he needs to. Now that his volume of e-mail has been drastically reduced, he scans the few messages in his inbox, takes a last gulp of coffee, and opens his classroom door to the sound of happy students.

Figure 8.3   Audacity is a free, open-source program that makes it easy to edit and mix your audio files.

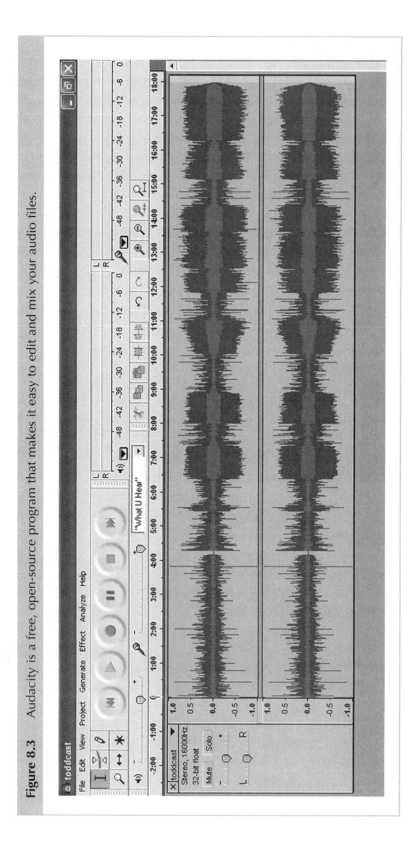

References

Allison, P. (2005, April 24). The chicken and the egg. *Weblogs & wikis & feeds, oh my!* Retrieved November 4, 2005, from http://www.nycwp.org/paulallison/2005/04/24#a34

Barrett, H. (2004). *Versions of my online portfolios.* Retrieved September 25, 2005, from http://electronicportfolios.org/myportfolio/versions.html

Bischoff, M. (2005). *Esc from the world! Weblog and podcasts about software and technology by teenage geek Matthew Bischoff.* Retrieved November 7, 2005, from http://matthewbischoff.com/

Brooks, S. (2005, April 18). *iPod in educations.* Retrieved April 18, 2005, from http://www.edugadget.com/2005/04/18/ipod-lessons-for-all-of-us/

Brooks, S. (2005, May 7). *Flickr creative commons.* Retrieved September 25, 2005, from http://www.edugadget.com/2005/05/07/flickr-creative-commons/

Carvin, A. (2005, February 1). *Tim Berners-Lee: Weaving a semantic web.* Retrieved September 25, 2005, from http://www.digitaldivide.net/articles/view.php?ArticleID=20

Cayahoga County Library. (2005). *Welcome to our education furl.* Retrieved November 5, 2005, from www.cuyahogalibrary.com/furl/educationfurl.htm

COSTP (California Open Source Textbook Project). (2002). Retrieved November 4, 2005, from http://www.opensourcetext.org/

Davis, A. (2005). *The write weblog: Who says elementary students can't blog?* Retrieved September 25, 2005, from http://itc.blogs.com/thewriteweblog/2004/11/who_says_elemen.html

Downes, S. (2005, July 16). *Stephen's Web: Principles for evaluating Websites.* Retrieved September 25, 2005, from http://www.downes.ca/cgi-bin/page.cgi?db=post&q=crdate=1121531748&format=full

Educause Learning Initiative. (2005, May). *7 things you should know about social bookmarking.* Retrieved November 5, 2005, from http://www.educause.edu/ir/library/pdf/ELI7001.pdf

Eide Neurolearning Blog. (2005, March 2). *Brain of the blogger.* Retrieved September 25, 2005, from http://eideneurolearningblog.blogspot.com/2005/03/brain-of-blogger.html

FCC Consumer and Governmental Affairs Bureau. (2003, September 17). *Children's Internet Protection Act.* Retrieved September 25, 2005, from http://www.fcc.gov/cgb/consumerfacts/cipa.html

Fox, S. (2005, October 5). Reports: Demographics. *Pew/Internet: Pew Internet & American life project.* Retrieved November 13, 2005, from http://www.pewinternet.org/PPF/r/165/report_display.asp

Freidman, T. (2005). *The world is flat: A brief history of the twenty-first century.* New York: Farr, Strauss and Giroux.

Ganley, B. (2004a, October). *bgblogging: October 2004 archives.* Retrieved September 25, 2005, from http://mt.middlebury.edu/middblogs/ganley/bgblogging/2004_10.html#004423

Ganley, B. (2004b, November). *bgblogging: November 2004 archives.* Retrieved September 25, 2005, from http://mt.middlebury.edu/middblogs/ganley/bgblogging/2004_11.html#005353

Giles, J. (2005). *Internet encyclopaedias go head to head.* Retrieved December 15, 2005, from http://www.nature.com/nature/journal/v438/n7070/full/438900a.html

Gillmor, D. (2005). The Read-Write Web. *We the media.* Retrieved September 25, 2005, from http://www.authorama.com/we-the-media-3.html

Glogowski, K. (2005, May 15). Writing vs. blogging (Part 2). In *Blog of proximal development* [Blog archive]. Retrieved September 25, 2005, from http://www.teachandlearn.ca/blog/2005/05/15/writing-vs-blogging-part-2/

Graham, J. (2004, December 14). Google's library plan "a huge help." *USA Today.* Retrieved September 26, 2005, from http://www.usatoday.com/money/industries/technology/2004–12–14-google-usat_x.htm

Halavais, A. (2004, August 29). *The Isuzu experiment.* Retrieved September 25, 2005, from http://alex.halavais.net/news/index.php?p=794

Hoffman, T. (2005, June 24). NECC talking points: Blogs as resources. *ed-tech insider.* Retrieved November 3, 2005, from http://www.eschoolnews. com/eti/2005/06/000877.php

Hunt, B. (2005). *Bud's blog experiment.* Retrieved November 2, 2005, fromhttp://budtheteacher.typepad.com/bud_the_teacher/

Jakes, D. (2005, May 10). *The strength of weak ties: Sandburg meets flickr.* Retrieved September 25, 2005, from http://jakespeak.blogspot.com/2005/05/sandburg-meets-flickr.html

Kidd, S. M. (2002). *The secret life of bees.* New York: Penguin.

Kosman, R. (2005, January 8). Are blogs the new journalism? *O'Reilly Developer Weblogs.* Retrieved September 25, 2005, from http://www.oreillynet.com/pub/wlg/6172

Kuropatwa, D. (2005, March 20). *Pre-Cal 40S: HERE!! HERE!!* Retrieved September 25, 2005, from http://pc40s.blogspot.com/2005/03/here-here.html

Lenhart, A., Fallows, D., & Horrigan, J. (2004, February 29). Reports: Online activities & pursuits. *Pew /Internet: Pew Internet & American life project.* Retrieved November 13, 2005, from www.pewinternet.org/PPF/r/113/report_display.asp

Levine, A. (2004, September 23). *Rip. Mix. Learn . . . The digital generation, social technologies, and learning.* A presentation for the Training Expo Partners

Conference, September 23, 2004. Retrieved November 14, 2005, from http://graphite.mcli.dist.maricopa.edu/emerging/wiki?RipMixLearn

McDowell, D. (2005, May 29). *About this project.* Retrieved November 4, 2005, from http://www.ahistoryteacher.com/holocaust/tiki-index.php?page=About+this+Project

National Education Technology Plan. (2005). Retrieved September 25, 2005, from http://www.nationaledtechplan.org/theplan/ANationontheMove .asp

National Endowment for the Arts. (2004, July 8). *Literary reading in dramatic decline, according to National Endowment for the Arts survey.* Retrieved November 10, 2005, from www.nea.gov/news/news04/ReadingAt Risk.html

NetDay News. (2005, March 8). *NetDay's 2004 survey results show 58 percent of students have cell phones, 60 percent email or IM adults on a weekly basis.* Retrieved September 25, 2005, from http://www.netday.org/news_2004_survey_results.htm

Olofson, C. (1999, December). Just the (meaningful) facts. *Fast Company, 30.* Retrieved November 13, 2005, from http://www.fastcompany.com/magazine/30/futurist.html

Paulina's Club. (2005, May 5). Retrieved on November 3, 2005, from http://itc.blogs.com/paulina/2005/05/our_lives_at_jh.html

Pein, C. (2005, January/February). Blog-gate. *Columbia Journalism Review.* Retrieved November 13, 2005, from http://www.cjr.org/issues/2005/1/pein-blog.asp

Prensky, M. (2001a). *Digital natives, digital immigrants.* Retrieved September 25, 2005, from www.marcprensky.com/writing/Prensky%20-%20Digital%20Natives,%20Digital%20Immigrants%20-%20Part1.pdf

Prensky, M. (2001b). The games generations: How learners have changed. In *Digital game-based learning.* Retrieved September 25, 2005, from http://www.marcprensky.com/writing/Prensky%20-%20Ch2-Digital%20Game-Based%20Learning.pdf

Prensky, M. (2004). *The emerging online life of the digital native: What they do differently because of technology, and how they do it.* Retrieved December 30, 2004, from http://www.marcprensky.com/writing/Prensky-The_Emerging_Online_Life_of_the_Digital_Native-03.pdf

Rheingold, H. (2004, November 4). *M-learning 4 generation txt?* Retrieved September 25, 2005, from http://www.thefeaturearchives.com/101157 .html

Rushkoff, D. (2004, October, 10). *Renaissance prospects.* Retrieved September 25, 2005, from http://www.itconversations.com/shows/detai1243 .html

Schwartz, J. (2004, December 28). The internet: Blogs provide raw details from scene of the disaster. *The New York Times.* Retrieved December 28, 2004, from http://www.nytimes.com/2004/12/28/technology/28 blogs.html? ex=1261890000&en=861d90080b50622f&ei=5090&partner= rssuserland

The secret life of bees: Questions for the author. (2002, September 26). Retrieved September 25, 2005, from http://weblogs.hcrhs.k12.nj.us/bees/discuss/msgReader$217?mode=topic&y=2002&m=9&d=27

Siemens, G. (2002, December 1). The art of blogging. *elearnspace: Everything elearning.* Retrieved September 26, 2005, from http://www.elearn space.org/Articles/blogging_part_1.htm

Siemens, G. (2005, March 3). *About: Description of connectivism.* Retrieved March 10, 2005, from http://www.connectivism.ca/about

Smith, K. (2004, March 30). *CCCC waves and ripples.* Retrieved September 25, 2005, from http://www.mchron.net/site/edublog_comments.php?id=P2636_0_13_0

Thatcher, M. (2005, March 15). The back page: Q & A with Chris Dede. *School CEO: The Newsletter for K-12 Technology Leaders.* Retrieved November 14, 2005, from http://www.techlearning.com/story/showArticle.jhtml?articleID=60407857

Vargas, E. (2004, December 30). Internet phenomenon provides unique insight into peoples' thoughts. *ABC News.* Retrieved November 13, 2005, from http://abcnews.go.com/WNT/PersonOfWeek/story?id=372266&page=1

Wales, J. (2004). Jimmy Wales. *Wikiquote.* Retrieved November 3, 2005, from http://en.wikiquote.org/wiki/Jimmy_Wales

Wenzloff, J. (2005, February 7). *Furl, furled, furling: Social on-line bookmarking for the masses.* Retrieved November 5, 2005, from http://www.class roomhelp.com/workshop/furl_guide.pdf

Wilson, T. (2005, September 24). Picking your battles. Retrieved December 4, 2005, from http://technosavvy.org/?p=307

Further Resources

BlogforAmerica. www.blogforamerica.com
Bud the Teacher. [Bud Hunt's blog] http://budtheteacher.typepad.com/bud_the_teacher/
The Dylan show. www.dylanverdi.com
Esc from the world! Weblog and podcast about software and technology by teenage geek Matthew Bischoff. www.matthewbischoff.com/blog
Greensboro101. www.greensbor0101.com
internic.com. www.internic.com [service for finding out who owns a Website]
Lewis Elementary. http://lewiselementary.org/
Northwest Voice. www.northwestvoice.com
Technorati.com. www.technorati.com [blog tracking site]
Tess's Weather Book. www.flickr.com/photos/wrichard/sets/96435/
Wikipedia. http://wikipedia.org

Index